A Guide to Great American Public Places

A GUIDE TO
GREAT AMERICAN PUBLIC PLACES

**A journey of discovery, learning and delight
in the public realm**

Gianni Longo

with a foreword by Deaderick C. Montague
and with an afterword by Tony Hiss

Unless otherwise credited, all photographs by Gianni Longo.

The writing and publication of this book was
sponsored by the Lyndhurst Foundation of
Chattanooga, Tennessee.

Published by Urban Initiatives, Inc.
Copyright © 1996 by Gianni Longo

Edited by Elizabeth Doberneck
Copy-edited by Emily Nunn
Cover and book design by Phil Collis
Cover photo © 1996 by Gianni Longo

ISBN: 0-936020-00-8

Printed in the U.S.A.

To Genny and Matt

The Lyndhurst Foundation

The Search for Great American Public Places, the publication of this book, and the Public Realm Recovery Project are sponsored by the Lyndhurst Foundation of Chattanooga, Tennessee. Rick Montague, the Foundation's president during its formative years in the late 70s and in the 80s, immersed himself and his colleagues in issues associated with the value of the public realm. The Search was supported in honor of his leadership. "Much of the impetus for supporting these programs," says Jack Murrah, the Foundation's current president, "comes from a sense of confusion, bordering on outrage, about what has happened to the public life of our towns and cities in the past 50 years. We want these programs to educate and inspire and to bring attention to what fosters the flowering of civil society in our cities and towns."

Acknowledgments

I wish to thank the Lyndhurst Foundation of Chattanooga for the continuous support of my work. For 16 years the Foundation has given me numerous opportunities to learn about the working of cities. In particular, I wish to thank Rick Montague, a close friend, for inspiring and influencing my work; Jack Murrah, for his laser-sharp leadership; and Alice Montague, for the great interest she has taken in our new undertaking, the Public Realm Recovery Project.

This book would not exist in its present form without the great efforts of my editors, Elizabeth Doberneck, who with unfailing hand has translated my suspiciously European sentence structures into English, and Emily Nunn, who has given it its final form. Special thanks go to Phil Collis, the book designer, for calmly dealing with another opinionated fellow-designer.

The preparation of this book has been a collaborative effort. Susan Stauber and Marilyn Rickman gathered preliminary information on each site and Jay Hathaway and Jenny Kim spent long hours in the library researching subjects all too often elusive. Jennifer Corazzo is helping with the book's promotion and distribution.

Friends have provided support. Suzanne and Henry Lennard have offered, with their International Making Cities Livable conferences, a forum for trying out ideas, while providing encouragement and frank criticism. Jamie Greene, a partner in the American Communities Partnership, has patiently accommodated the impossible schedule of the last six months of the book's production. Many other friends have encouraged and counseled me: Ned Smyth, George Negroponte, Igor Jozsa, Noni Pratt, Bob McNulthy, and Nora York.

Finally, I wish to thank all who responded to the call for nominations in the Search for Great American Public Places and those who assisted us in gathering on-site information for each place. Without their contributions this publication would not exist. ∎

Table of Contents

Acknowledgments

About the Search   XI

The Panel   XIII

Foreword by Rick Montague   XV

Introduction   1

Visions   9
Grace Marchant Garden, San Francisco, California
Socrates Sculpture Park, Queens, New York
The West Side Community Garden, Manhattan,
   New York

Connections   17
Golden Gate National Recreational Area,
   San Francisco, California
Lithia Park, Ashland, Oregon
Riverwalk, Chattanooga, Tennessee
Appalachian National Scenic Trail
Union Square Market, Manhattan, New York

Pleasurable Rides   29
St. Charles Avenue Streetcars, New Orleans, Louisiana
San Francisco Bay Ferries, San Francisco, California
Brooklyn Bridge Promenade, Brooklyn, New York
Union Station, Los Angeles, California
Pioneer Courthouse Square, Portland, Oregon
Blue Ridge Parkway, Virginia; North Carolina

Small Towns   43
Four Towns:
   Nantucket, Massachusetts
   New Harmony, Indiana
   Portsmouth, New Hampshire
   Greenwich, New York
Charleston, South Carolina
Acoma and Taos Pueblos, New Mexico

Planned Communities   55
Yorkship Village, Camden, New Jersey
Diggs Town, Norfolk, Virginia
Seaside, Florida

Endangered and in Transition   65
Times Square, Manhattan, New York
The French Quarter, New Orleans, Louisiana
Coney Island and **Jacob Riis Park**, Brooklyn, New York

Waterfronts   73
Oceanfront Walk, Venice, California
Ocean Drive, Miami Beach, Florida
Battery Park City Esplanade, Manhattan, New York

Main Streets and Places of Commerce 83
Country Club Plaza, Kansas City, Missouri
Faneuil Hall Marketplace, Boston, Massachusetts
Newbury Street, Boston, Massachusetts
Xenia Avenue and **Main Street**,
  Yellow Springs, Ohio
  Madison, Indiana

Outdoor Living Rooms 95
Bryant Park, Manhattan, New York
Post Office Square, Boston, Massachusetts
Washington Square, San Francisco, California
The Promenade and Plaza, Rockefeller Center
  Manhattan, New York
Low Memorial Library Steps, Columbia University,
  Manhattan, New York

Public Squares 107
The Green, New Haven, Connecticut
The Plaza, Santa Fe, New Mexico
El Pueblo de Los Angeles, Los Angeles, California
Courthouse Squares:
  Oxford, Mississippi
  Sidney, Ohio

Public Buildings 119
Los Angeles Central Library, Los Angeles, California
Grand Terminals:
  Grand Central Terminal, Manhattan, New York
  South Station, Boston, Massachusetts
The Atrium, Franklin Institute, Philadelphia,
  Pennsylvania

Farmers' Markets 129
Pike Place Market, Seattle, Washington
Three Farmers' Markets:
  Central Market, Lancaster, Pennsylvania
  Market Square, Roanoke, Virginia
  Italian Market, Philadelphia, Pennsylvania

Turning Points 137
The Lawn, University of Virginia, Charlottesville,
Virginia
Grand Parks:
  Golden Gate Park, San Francisco, California
  Central Park, Manhattan, New York
  Prospect Park, Brooklyn, New York
Vietnam Veterans Memorial, Washington, D.C.
Oriole Park at Camden Yards, Baltimore, Maryland

Afterword: *The Search Is On*, by Tony Hiss 149

Getting There 154

Some Readings, A Bibliography 157

About the Search

The 60 places included in this publication were selected from over 200 locations nominated in a program called the Search for Great American Public Places.

The program began in June 1994 with a call to architects, planners, artists, writers, elected officials, and developers around the country to name and describe their favorite public places. The definition of the term public place was deliberately left open. The list of locations generated produced exciting discoveries, but it is just a beginning, the tip of the iceberg, in our effort to understand and describe the good design and the life manifested in this nation's public spaces.

This publication marks the completion of the first Search for Great American Public Places and the beginning of a new phase of the program—the Public Realm Recovery Project. The Recovery Project will continue the Search while also identifying ways to further the continued enjoyment and protection of public places in our communities.

The Search is still on. We invite you to submit a list of your favorite places—small and large, used or neglected—and to share with us the reasons for your selections.

To make your nominations write to:
The Public Realm Recovery Project
530 West 25th Street
New York, New York 10001
e-mail: placeprjct@aol.com

Greenwich, New York.

Photo by Daniel T. Seginak.

The Panel

The panel assembled to sift through more than 200 entries collected through the Search for Great American Public Places and select the best among them, at Seaside, Florida, in February of 1995. The panel included Laurie Beckelman of the Public Theater; Robert S. Davis, developer of Seaside, Florida; Barbara Flanagan, architect and journalist; Jan Gehl, senior professor of urban design at the Royal Academy of Fine Arts, Copenhagen, Denmark; Paul Goldberger, chief cultural correspondent for *The New York Times*; Tony Hiss, author of *The Experience of Place*; Peter Katz, author of *The New Urbanism*; Daniel Kemmis, mayor of Missoula, Montana, and author of *Community and the Politics of Place* and *The Good City and the Good Life*; James H. Kunstler, author of *The Geography of Nowhere*; Rick Montague, chairman of the Southern Environmental Law Center, Chattanooga, Tennessee; and Dick Swett, architect and New Hampshire congressman.

The selection process was a difficult one. The panel looked not only at the formal and aesthetic qualities of each place, but also at their ability to bring people together for the face-to-face contact that is essential to a healthy society. These entries suggest an intriguing and inclusive definition of public places and offer a vast inventory of solutions and strategies that can be used by other communities. ∎

The Panel (from left):
Tony Hiss, Gianni Longo,
Rick Montague, Barbara Flanagan,
James H. Kunstler, Peter Katz,
Paul Goldberger, Laurie Beckelman,
Dick Swett, Robert S. Davis,
Daniel Kemmis, Jan Gehl.

Photo by Elizabeth Doberneck.

Foreword

Rick Montague

Pinpointing the origin of my love for public spaces
and my curiosity about them is impossible, but
it began early in life, and my interest has continued
to grow—especially thanks to my experience as the
former president of the Lyndhurst Foundation,
where we worked to strengthen the public realm and
to generate excitement for our own city of
Chattanooga, Tennessee.

After I was born I lived in an apartment building in
a small Chattanooga neighborhood. My brother and I
could walk not only to grammar school, but also to
the doctor's office and the pharmacy—for chocolate
ice-cream cones or limeades—to the grocery store
down the street, and even to the park. The
sidewalks, with their octagonal paving stones and
massive oak trees, were where we first learned to
know something about people who were different
from our family.

Two of our regular destinations had a powerful
effect upon me. In their visual and textural richness
and the magisterial mystery of their design, these
places were as important to me as any painting I
have ever seen, any book I have read, or any piece
of music I know. One was the flowing marble
staircase leading up to the Ochs Memorial Temple,
around the corner from our apartment. For a young
child, playing on it was like wading in a rushing river;
waves seemed to tumble down from the building's
imposing doors.

The other was the post office and lobby of the
Federal Court Building, a sumptuous Art Deco edifice
built during the Depression by the W.P.A. Its
grandeur, the elegance of its architecture and
appointments, communicated—even to a child of
four—a respect for and an unshakable belief in
abstractions like democracy, government, and
America. The dark walls, the eloquent curves, the

*Musicians and other performing
artists contribute to the liveliness
of the streets around Pike Place
Market, in Seattle. Some old-timers,
however, complain that, despite the
effort to maintain the market's
integrity, an element of adventure
has been lost.*

The Walnut Street Bridge, in Chattanooga, once slated for demolition, has been restored as a vital pedestrian link between the two shores of the Tennessee River.

lettering, even the solidity of the mailboxes fashioned out of chrome and heavy stainless steel inspired me to want to play a part in what I would someday come to know as our civil society.

Our family visited the French Quarter, in New Orleans, one spring vacation. It was dank, dirty, and smelly—as it is today—but even then I was aware of its timeless intricacy—from the shadow of St. Louis Cathedral, the cobbled alleyways, and forbidding metal gates to the striped awnings of the Café du Monde, where the smell of the Mississippi River vied with the aroma of the potent Louisiana coffee.

A few years later, we spent the night in New York City at the old Astor Hotel, where I squeezed onto the balcony overlooking Times Square to gawk at a sight unlike any I had ever seen; the endless, garishly lit crowds of people held me magnetized until the early hours of the morning.

With the birth of yet another brother, our family moved to a larger home in one of the nearby suburban towns. Now, of course, we drove to school, to church, and everywhere else. We spent an increasing amount of our time in private schools and clubs; our social distance from the city grew out of proportion to the traffic-free commute from home to downtown. Without realizing it, we and nearly all of our contemporaries were insulating ourselves, gravitating toward private institutions, lending our

energies to organizations that doubtless made for a
more attractive city and more effective social
agencies, but which were largely removed from the
public realm—geographically, socially, economically.
We may have been building stronger bricks, but we
were neglecting the chemistry of the mortar and the
craftsmanship of the joints.

In my fourth year at the University of Virginia, I
lived on the Lawn—the central quadrangle of the
school created by Thomas Jefferson. As its founder
intended, this experience marked my life with a
curiosity about and hunger for architectural genius,
for the power of place and what it communicates to
an individual about one's part in a society that is
larger and more complex than one's immediate
circle of acquaintances. I am not the first to
question whether our current social estrangement
and hostility is not in part a product of our national
denigration of beautiful, inspiring, and enduring
design in public spaces.

Those of us who have joined the search for great
American public spaces want to somehow reverse
the sorry work of architects, road builders, and
parking-lot providers who conspired to rip apart the
fabric that held city and town and their people
together. We want to reclaim these places, not for
nostalgic or aesthetic reasons alone, but because
they belong to all of us, and because we too have a

*Street entertainers delight visitors
at New Orleans' Jackson Square.*

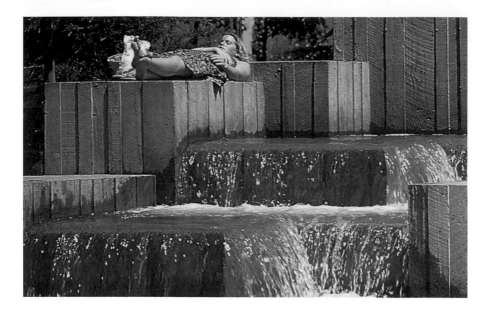

voice in shaping what effects us so powerfully.

I remember that the first time I heard the term "public realm" was from the urban designer Stroud Watson, then head of the Remote Design Studio and of a staff of eager architecture students from the University of Tennessee. He had come to Chattanooga because the Lyndhurst Foundation believed that the city's buildings and their relationship to our streets and parks could, over time, shape people's attitudes toward our downtown and riverfront. This notion, as old as the idea of the city itself, was expressed most eloquently by the Greeks, but it was a message forgotten as we were all moving—by car—to the suburbs.

In the years that followed, Lyndhurst, the city, the county, and other major contributors created new plazas, parks, and squares in Chattanooga, as well as a host of amenities along the banks of the Tennessee River. These investments gave Chattanoogans a chance to reinvent a tradition of living and celebrating together in public places that bore no scars of race, class, or neighborhood barriers. They created a new spirit of tolerance, energy, and curiosity.

With Chattanooga's good fortune in mind, Jack Murrah, my successor at the Foundation, Gianni Longo, one of our favorite project directors of the preceding decade, and I determined to find a way to encourage others to rediscover not only the shining and grand examples of public spaces but also

uniquely local and eccentric ones. What we devised was the Search for Great American Public Places—a celebration of architectural spaces whose character encourages and enhances the dying concept of citizenship and community-building. Our hope is that this book will excite others to value the special places in their home communities—to protect them and learn from them, and when possible, to create new ones, knowing that such spaces are not only filled with mystery, pleasure, and delight but also foster a sense of membership in the larger society. ■

Pioneer Courthouse Square in Portland, Oregon, is the stage for hundreds of events that have re-established residents' trust in downtown.

The Rotunda, at the north end of the Lawn, originally housed the University of Virginia's main library.

Introduction

The Search for Great American Public Places has taken me on a two-year journey, during which I discovered new locations, revisited familiar ones, and learned what makes each of them special. I returned excited but also sobered by the present state of the nation's public places. In this magnificent revival period, squares, parks, riverfronts, and public buildings have been renovated and are better kept than before, and they are brimming with people who display a freedom and easiness that one rarely encountered in such places just few years ago. Unfortunately, for each one restored or built anew there are many, often just blocks away, that require care and attention.

More then ever, however, public places are in danger of extinction, and the forces that have contributed to their physical decline show no signs of abating. A nation of cities continues to be transformed into a nation of suburbs, where only the most affluent live. (By 1990, 60 percent of the urban population lived in suburbs, where income levels were 30 percent higher than in central cities.) And as jobs and opportunities have migrated to suburbs, central cities have been left to provide more services to a poorer population, with fewer resources to do so. In addition, we have increasingly become a nation in which private automobiles are the primary means of transportation—despite the negative impact they have on the environment.

The building surge that accompanied the great growth of suburbs has produced neither memorable public places nor even mediocre ones. Huge sprawls of housing subdivisions and business centers have sprung up at highway intersections and around older metropolitan areas, but they are built with cars in mind, with no intention of encouraging social and public use. Highway ramps, 10-lane arterial roads,

Street theater, spontaneous or organized, has become a key component of our cities' public life.

1

On weekends, Jacob Riis Park, in Brooklyn, New York, becomes the place for jam sessions, soccer games, and barbeques.

cul-de-sacs, office parks, and shopping malls surrounded by immense parking lots create a hostile environment of wasted space that seems appropriate for two lonely activities only: jogging and driving.

And since entire generations have grown up in suburbs, many young citizens, having never experienced the city as an exciting, diverse, nurturing place, have no emotional ties to it; in fact, many young suburbanites believe cities are dangerous and stay away from them completely—a situation that can only worsen as the years go by.

Because the suburbs have failed to create new types of public places and sites located in older parts of cities have declined, the rich diversity of the public environment—forever the symbol of a community's aesthetic and social values—has been all but lost. And not only have our efforts to revive this diversity fallen short, but our supply of successful and inspiring models to emulate is also dwindling.

Major sites in central locations (urban riverfronts, downtown plazas and parks, fashionable shopping streets, and historic districts) have received lavish investments and been the focus of innovative management efforts that sustain their vitality, but smaller and less central places (neighborhood streets and parks, playgrounds, small amenities, gardens, neighborhood squares, and commercial centers) have suffered and declined. In fact, many

small public spaces—which have become the victims of redevelopment, privatization, and neglect—are disappearing altogether.

By day, Coney Island boardwalk belongs to old-timers and retirees; at night, gangs take over.

To stem this decline and loss we need a different kind of leadership, one capable of harnessing the various interests that have had an impact, both good and bad, on the survival of public places. But a peculiar quality of the public realm is that it is the realm of freedom. We can't (nor do we want to) control who occupies it, how they dress, or how they behave. Similarly, we have little control over what private developers, lenders, traffic engineers, or citizens can do to the public realm (like demolish buildings, build new ones, enlarge streets, or vandalize them). As the 60 cases presented in this book show, leaders and citizens must share a common sense of purpose in order to preserve and restore public places.

Twenty of the sites included in this book exist only because someone—an individual or a civic group— took a stand to protect them from demolition or made the effort to create them from scratch. Without their leadership and alertness we might have a multistory parking garage instead of Pioneer Courthouse Square in Portland, Oregon, or a 54-story building sitting atop a gutted Grand Central Terminal, in Manhattan. We might have an urban-renewal wasteland instead of the extraordinary Pike Place Market, in Seattle, or a modern glass

The green roof of the underground parking garage on a typical summer's day. Post Office Square, in Boston, demonstrates that it is possible to look after the needs of drivers without sacrificing our sidewalks to massive above-ground parking garages.

Photo by Steve Dunwell. Courtesy of Friends of Post Office Square, Inc.

skyscraper in place of the beautifully refurbished Los Angeles Central Library. This watchful stance must continue, even after a place has been successfully renovated. As Charleston's Mayor Joseph P. Riley, Jr., has said, "If eternal vigilance is the price of liberty, eternal vigilance is also the price of a great city."

Creativity is the key to financing new places and restoring old ones. Fifteen more of the sites included here have been built or substantially upgraded through thoughtful collaboration between the public and private sectors. The construction of Post Office Square, in Boston, and the renovation of Bryant Park, in Manhattan, were paid for by local businesses who saw the value and virtues of creating a great public place in their front yards. Faneuil Hall Marketplace, which twenty years ago helped blaze the trail for new places and opportunities in downtown Boston, was the result of the entrepreneurial vision of its developer and of Boston mayor Kevin White. Cities can use consensus to master the resources to care for the public realm, even at times when those resources are minimal. On the strength of a shared sense of purpose, the Riverwalk along the Tennessee River, in Chattanooga, and Market Square, in

One measure of a public place's success is the ease with which people fit themselves into the scenery. Friends meet at Portland's Pioneer Courthouse Square (above): a man makes himself comfortable on the seawall in Miami's Lummus Park (below).

Definitions

The phrase public realm means different things to different people. Architects and planners tend to define it as the totality of the physical elements, buildings, amenities, and landscapes that together form what we see when we are in a city. For others, the public realm is the sphere of public activities, from the simplest act, like sitting on a bench watching people go by, to the most complex public interactions like community and social events, commercial transactions, and political rallies. To me the public realm implies the confluence of the two: the coming together of the form of a place with the activities that occur there. One cannot exist without the other. Although at different times in the book I make reference to specific formal aspects of a place or describe specific activities, the implication is always that the two elements, formal and social, work together.

Roanoke, have become catalysts for the transformation of public places in their respective communities. These strategies, which have been successful in central locations, must now be applied everywhere. It is a daunting task, but one we must face if we hope to restore the infrastructure of public places in our communities. The sixty places in this book show us how we can do that.

Throughout the two years I have spent on The Search for Great American Places, I have often been asked which of the sixty is my favorite. Although I am especially fond of several of them (the St. Charles Avenue streetcars, in New Orleans, for the sense of place they create; Diggs Town, in Norfolk, because it transformed a desperate housing project into a hopeful community; Charleston, because it is the most beautiful city in the country; Lithia Park, in Ashland, because it connects a city with the wilderness around it; and Bryant Park, for its spectacular metamorphosis), my answer to that question is: all of them. To me, all sixty places (or

rather the type of public space they represent) are part of an ideal city, to which every community in the country, large or small, should aspire. I hope that this book will inspire readers to start looking in their own communities for lost treasures, to do whatever it takes to protect them, and, ultimately, to enjoy them. ∎

—*Gianni Longo, New York, 1996.*

The roots of a dream

In the prologue to her book The Human Condition, *Hannah Arendt speaks with great eloquence of the longing humans have to escape their present surroundings. An example she uses is that of the launching of the first man-made spacecraft, in 1957, hailed by the contemporary press as "the first step toward escape from men's imprisonment to the earth." In that desire for "flight from the earth into the universe and from the world into the self," she sees the roots of modern world alienation. As the physical manifestation of our human condition and the repository of our social experience, cities are what we most long to escape. We have done that, quite successfully, for the last half century.*

This mass exodus has been propelled by the building of new highways, the availability of cheap fuel and land, the relentless promotion of the suburban lifestyle by car manufacturers, low interest loans, and the dream of building a different and better world. That dream has been interrupted by a rude awakening, however, as uniformity, alienation, and loneliness have become the symbols of suburban living, and traffic, congestion, and crime have brought to the suburbs what people had come there to escape.

Abandoned, older cities have turned ugly and unfamiliar to many. Places that have great history and beauty have been left to deteriorate, been torn down or privatized. The memory of past brilliance and excitement has faded away. To reconstruct what has been lost (their physical form and our sense of freedom in using them) will require a concerted effort on the part of citizens, leaders and institutions. The effort is, as Ms. Arendt would say, more than relevant "to the future of men." We believe the Search for Great American Public Places is a first, albeit small, step in that direction.

The Mermaid Parade is Coney Island's most popular event (right).

Photo by Matt Longo.

Visions

The places in this chapter are very different from each other, yet they have one thing in common: they were conceived and built by citizens who had the vision, inspiration, and drive to transform their surroundings. They are representative of the many citizen efforts that have transformed neglected corners of cities into imaginative, well-loved gardens, parks, and playgrounds.

The Grace Marchant Garden is the work of one woman who spent 35 years turning a San Francisco street into a lush oasis. In Queens, an artist came together with a community to transform an illegal dump site in their neighborhood into a sculpture garden, Socrates Sculpture Park. And Manhattan residents built the West Side Community Garden with their own hands and then fought to preserve it when the city sold the land out from under them. ■

Socrates Sculpture Park.

Sculpture by Marc di Suvero.
Photo by Barry Munger.

Grace Marchant Garden

San Francisco, California

Photo by L. Habegger.

Grace Marchant (pictured) left her mark on San Francisco; her garden, thirty years in the making, surrounds the Filbert Steps, at times becoming a narrow tunnel of green, at others an open meadow of brilliantly colored perennial flowers.

Bursting with hundreds of flowers, shrubs, and trees, the Grace Marchant Garden is a wild rambling affair surrounding the Filbert Steps in San Francisco. One woman's labor of love, it is a reminder that the making of the public realm is every citizen's business and that it can occur anywhere, even in a location as challenging as the Steps, a steep San Francisco street that becomes a flight of wooden stairs climbing Telegraph Hill.

When Grace Marchant moved to the corner of Napier Lane and Filbert Street in 1949, the hillside was littered with debris. She took it upon herself to clean it up and spent the rest of her life cultivating the garden that graces the steps today. Grace tended her plants wherever they grew, whether they lay on common ground or in someone else's yard. As a result, what began as a private garden has become a

Photo by D. Hoffman.

Locals have taken ownership of the garden; in 1985 they formed Friends of the Garden to protect and maintain it.

public one, where residents and visitors encounter a place of exuberant and sensual beauty, solitude and surprise in the middle of this large city. ■

A Touch of Eden

In creating her garden, Grace Marchant was very casual about property lines. One large section extended into the yard of a cottage whose owner wanted the land back in 1985 to build a larger house. When a permit for construction was granted, neighbors founded Friends of the Garden and took the issue of its preservation to City Hall and the Trust for Public Land. The Trust developed a plan to buy the cottage property and resell it with deed restrictions protecting the garden. To cover the difference between the purchase price and the much lower resale value of the restricted property, donations came in from garden lovers. With additional gifts from local corporations, foundations, and benefit events, the Trust exceeded its fund-raising goal, enabling it to buy the cottage and create an endowment to support the garden. Friends of the Garden have since taken over the maintenance of Grace Marchant's gardening vision.

The Filbert Steps—among the last of the wooden staircases that once served as public streets in San Francisco—connect Coit Tower, a popular tourist stop at the top of Telegraph Hill, with Sansome Street and the financial district, at the foot of the hill. Halfway down they are intersected by Napier Lane, one of the city's last wooden boardwalk streets, occupied by a row of cottages that miraculously escaped the 1906 fire.

"At the intersection of Filbert Street and Napier Lane, you can sit on a wooden bench and enjoy the lush greenery and the company of the neighborhood cats while taking in a breathtaking view of San Francisco Bay." Carolyn R. Shaffer, from her letter of nomination.

Socrates Sculpture Park

Queens, New York

Photo by Steven L. Cohen, Courtesy of Socrates Sculpture Park.

Socrates Sculpture Park is an outstanding example of how even the most neglected site can be successfully revived. Its site, which faces the northern tip of Roosevelt Island (just south of Hell Gate where the Harlem and East rivers meet), was once a marine terminal, but after 20 years of obsolescence it had become a polluted, illegal dumping ground and a frightening no-man's-land. Led by Marc di Suvero, whose enormous steel sculptures are in the collections of museums worldwide, hundreds of volunteers and residents of nearby neighborhoods worked side by side with artists for an entire year, picking up trash, leveling the grounds, planting grass and trees, spreading gravel, and painting rocks.

Today, Socrates Park is a renowned outdoor gallery, and the only place in the New York metropolitan area where large outdoor sculptures are routinely exhibited. Artists from all over the world present site-specific sculptures in semi-annual exhibitions, as well as dance, film, and video presentations.

But Socrates is more that just an outdoor museum; it is a true community park used by the people who built it—residents of the African-American, Hispanic, and Greek neighborhoods that surround the park—as an extension of their homes: a place for barbecues, parties, and gatherings, and a place to experience art in joyful and fun ways.

A confluence of interests brought Socrates to life. Artists in need of a place to show large sculptures and residents bent on eliminating a neighborhood

With the Manhattan skyline as its backdrop, the park offers an extraordinary setting for large-scale sculptures, like this one by Marc di Suvero.

Photo by Barry Munger.

Socrates Sculpture Park's large open space is bordered by rock gardens, walls, gravel walkways, wild grass, and boulders lining the banks of the East River. Sculpture in foreground by Allison Slon.

eyesore created a large, rough-edged, minimalist park that works well for all involved and serves to remind the community of its own powers of vision. ■

Courtesy of Socrates Sculpture Park.

Senegalese drummers and dancers perform at the 1994 opening of "Bongo Park," in which an international array of artists presented sculptures dealing with the theme of nature.

Artistic Independence

Socrates Sculpture Park formally became part of New York City's Department of Parks and Recreation in May of 1994, the first addition of park-land in more than a decade. Although this affiliation with the City safeguards Socrates park's future, ninety percent of its $150,000 annual budget is still provided for by private sources, with arts grants from the state and city providing the other ten. Community volunteers continue to run the park themselves.

The West Side Community Garden

Manhattan, New York

Landscape architect R. Terry Schnadelbach translated the community gardeners' wishes into a design that won the Philip N. Winslow Landscape Design Award from the Parks Council.

The West Side Community Garden, created when residents of a block on West 89th Street in Manhattan took over a lot that had been cleared for urban renewal and then abandoned, is part of a phenomenon that has led to the creation of hundreds of other such green spots throughout New York— in effect establishing an alternative park system in the city. More than 1,000 of these oases cover 125 acres of vacant lots in all five boroughs, involving tens of thousands of volunteers.

The West Side's design has been widely imitated. Half garden, half park, it is divided into a working section, where flowers and vegetables are grown in rows of raised plots, and a more formal one that includes meandering landscaped paths, flowering perennial borders, and a rock garden. In the summer this area, which also contains an amphitheater and secluded places with benches, is the social hub of the block.

The West Side Community Garden was originally a vacant lot used as a temporary landfill; it was nicknamed "strip city" by local residents because cars were brought there to be stripped.

From dawn to dusk, children play and neighbors chat under the vine-covered trellises, gardeners tend their plots, and teenagers hang out on the benches. It is a quintessential gathering place, one that fulfills two critical needs of people living in crowded cities: to socialize and to grow things. ■

The West Side Community Garden is a volunteer organization, with an elected board of directors, elected committees, and no paid staff. All planning, planting, transplanting, pruning, cleanup, and fund raising is done by members and volunteers.

West Side Story

The story of the West Side Community Garden is full of twists and turns. Started by residents in 1976 on a city-owned lot, within two years the garden covered 35,000 square feet of space with 130 thriving vegetable and flower gardens, including vegetable plots tended by schoolchildren. In 1977, the city sold the lot to two developers, whose subsequent proposal for luxury townhouses provided the neighborhood with nothing to replace the garden. A controversy ensued, but after the Trust for Public Land became involved in 1982, a compromise was reached.

The developers agreed to set aside 17,500 square feet of their site for a new West Side Community Garden, to be built according to the gardeners' design. They also provided $100,000 in cash and in-kind services—an amount matched by garden member grants and contributions—and the city showed support by not taxing the land. The West Side Community Garden reopened in the spring of 1989 as a permanent garden, owned and managed by volunteers.

Connections

A s our cities continue to grow and the surrounding rural areas are transformed into suburbs, the strong connection that once existed between the rural and the urban—a link vital to the formation of a mutually supportive, self-reliant aggregate with its own physical identity and indigenous economy—is being lost. Each of the places in this chapter embraces a regional view of the public realm and provides a place where the two worlds of the urban and rural can meet.

Both the Golden Gate National Recreational Area, in San Francisco, and Lithia Park, in Ashland, Oregon, although located in communities of differing sizes, link a city with its natural surroundings. The Chattanooga Riverwalk connects Chattanooga not only with the Tennessee River but also with its past as a city nurtured by the river trade. The Appalachian National Scenic Trail provides the millions who live on the eastern seaboard with easy access to the region's unspoiled natural areas. The Union Square Market in Manhattan connects New York City with its farming hinterland and the bounty of products cultivated there. ∎

With the Golden Gate Bridge arching above, a fisherman tries the water at Fort Point, an 1853 coastal fortification built to protect the narrow entrance of San Francisco Harbor.

Golden Gate
National Recreation Area

San Francisco, California

In San Francisco, the Golden Gate National Recreation Area begins at Aquatic Park on the northern edge of the city and extends west around the peninsula, encompassing the Presidio and Fort Point, overlooking the harbor, and the beaches, bluffs, and hiking trails of the western shore. Many of the sites are just blocks from San Francisco neighborhoods; all are accessible by public transportation.

The Golden Gate National Recreation Area is a vast and varied coastal preserve that connects residents of the San Francisco Bay Area with some of the region's key historic and natural features—the Pacific Ocean, the Bay, the Golden Gate Strait, the Marin Headlands, and the Golden Gate Bridge. Its 38,000 acres contain wilderness preserves, historic sites, museums, a chic urban park, beaches, farms, and ruins. Residents and visitors use and enjoy it as a source of entertainment, fresh air, and natural beauty.

To comprehend the wisdom of its design, one needs to see it from the air: the contiguous sites

From the lookout at Fort Funston, the immensity of the National Recreation Area's terrain is evident; 45 times larger than Central Park, 38 times larger than Golden Gate Park, it is a place of sudden fogs, prolonged sunsets, and sustained wild winds.

The Fight for the Marin Headlands

The fight to preserve the Marin Headlands from development was an important step toward the establishment of the Golden Gate National Recreation Area. The Headlands were originally occupied by a military battery protecting the entrance to San Francisco Bay. By the end of World War II, however, the fortifications had become obsolete, and the Headlands, with their extraordinary natural beauty, had become a prime target for development.

In 1965, Marin County approved plans for a new city of 25,000 inhabitants, to be called Marincello. Citizen groups fought Marincello in the courts, in public hearings, and in the press, until 1970, when the California Supreme Court ruled against the project and its sponsor withdrew. Advocates formed People for a Golden Gate National Recreation Area to persuade the federal government to turn it into a national park and to insure that the Headlands would be protected forever. In 1972, congress established the Golden Gate National Recreation Area, of which the Headlands became a part.

form a thin coastal border that extends for miles around the San Francisco peninsula, across the water, and up the western coast of Marin County, at once protecting and making accessible the priceless array of historic and natural sites. The recreation area would not exist if it had not been for the Bay Area leaders and citizens who opposed developments in the Marin Headlands in the late 1960s. The conflict, which lasted for years, led to the intervention of the Federal Government and to the establishment of the Golden Gate National Recreation Area as the country's first National Urban Park, a designation that recognizes how tightly the urban and rural features of the region are interwoven. It also led to the creation of the Trust for Public Land, which has since become one of the country's major forces in land preservation. The fact that 18 million people visit this grand tract of land each year is the finest tribute to the vision and perseverance of those who saw the value of protecting it for posterity. ∎

The six million people who live in this region are never far from the canyons and redwood groves of Marin County. Extending 30 miles up the coast, this section contains the Muir Woods and the Marin Headlands, an area of primordial beauty and a vestige of what the region looked like before human settlement.

Lithia Park

Ashland, Oregon

Although much smaller than San Francisco's Golden Gate National Recreation Area, Lithia Park in the small town of Ashland, Oregon, functions in a similar way, connecting the town center with Mt. Ashland, which is more than a mile away, and creating a preserve for a rich variety of trees found in the Oregon woods, within a stone's throw of Ashland's residential neighborhoods.

Lithia Park is shaped like an arrowhead, its point buried in the heart of downtown, where it takes the form of an urban green the size of a

Chester Corry's landscape designs for the park preserved and embellished the woods and hills with native mountain flowers, ferns, and trees.

small city block. Surrounded on three sides by downtown office buildings, residences, and a well-known Shakespearean theater complex, this section serves as Ashland's town square. To the north the park drops its formality, making a transition from downtown park to almost primeval forest, thanks to the wisdom of landscape designer John McLaren (the guiding genius of San Francisco's Golden Gate Park) and to the perseverance of Chester Corry, who, as park superintendent from 1937 to 1969, insisted on planting native flora.

As the park spreads uptown over 100 acres, the trees grow denser and the paths narrower, the formal flower beds and lawns become a rough carpet of ferns and shrubs, and Ashland Creek, previously tamed by graceful man-made waterfalls, is allowed to run wild. The park becomes a forest, the walk a hike, and yet one is still well within the boundaries of Ashland's residential neighborhoods.

Lithia Park is a powerful presence in Ashland, which is impressive considering the town is surrounded by pristine forests and white-water rivers. Amidst this natural abundance, it is special

Near the center of downtown, Lithia Park takes the form of a traditional town green.

precisely because it is an integral part of the town itself, not just another element of the town's visual landscape. ■

The Lower Duck Pond marks the beginning of the park's graceful transition from tame urban green to apparent wilderness.

Come to the Chautauqua

Lithia Park has its origins in the Chautauquas of the 1890s. These summertime camp meetings, often held outdoors under tents, were popular in small towns across the country, entertaining citizens with concerts, plays, and lectures. Every summer for two weeks, Ashland was the site of the Southern Oregon Chautauqua, attended by people from around the state. It was held on grounds just outside of town, and eventually a permanent wooden structure, called the Tabernacle, was built to house the festivities. Though owned by the Chautauqua Association, these grounds were open to the public, served as the nucleus of Lithia Park, and gave Ashland the distinction of having the first public park in southern Oregon.

Riverwalk

Chattanooga, Tennessee

The Fishing Piers, endorsed by the Vision 2000 process (a series of city-wide meetings), attract a broad range of people.

For many years, the lush banks of the majestic Tennessee River were all but inaccessible to most Chattanooga residents. In 1986, however, a seven-mile landscaped path called Riverwalk was built, and it quickly became a catalyst for the development of some of Chattanooga's most popular recreational facilities, as well as a great social equalizer. Once, only a wealthy few with homes on the banks of the Tennessee could enjoy its beauty; today, now that the Riverwalk has reconnected the city's diverse neighborhoods to the river, every citizen can.

Fishing piers, parks, plazas, homes, offices, shops, restaurants, and the Tennessee Aquarium (the world's largest fresh water aquarium) have all been built on or around the Walk, which will extend for twenty miles on both sides of the river when completed. These new facilities have none of the race or class distinctions attached to many of the older places in the community, and they attract citizens and tourists of every stripe.

Since nearly everyone in Chattanooga seems to have gotten involved in some aspect of the Riverwalk project, it has the stamp of community ownership. Thanks to ad-hoc coalitions of citizens, government and private-sector leaders, and local foundations, which have supplied financial, political, and technical support, the Riverwalk and the many public facilities it has spawned have become symbolic of the city's civic and physical renaissance. Chattanooga, once a sleepy Southern town, has transformed itself into one of the country's most progressive communities. ∎

"The River Is Everybody's Business"

The degree of community participation in the Chattanooga Riverwalk's conception and implementation has made it unique among the many riverfront projects of the past two decades. The bold idea of creating one continuous path along twenty miles of the Tennessee river was first formulated in 1983 by a city- and county-appointed citizen task force. Vision 2000, a series of community-wide brainstorm sessions aimed at improving Chattanooga's quality of life, adopted the idea a year later and supplied the impetus for its implementation. Two nonprofit organizations, the RiverCity Company and Chattanooga Venture, established as a result of Vision 2000, contributed in major ways to the creation of the Riverwalk and its associated developments.

A postscript: ReVision 2000, a second series of public meetings conducted nine years later, in 1993, reconfirmed Chattanooga's commitment to the river and emphasized the environment as a central theme in the city's continued revitalization.

Courtesy of River Valley Partners, Inc.

The C.B. Robinson segment of the Riverwalk, which includes fishing piers, playgrounds, open meadows, and a multi-purpose meeting space, has become the most popular park in Chattanooga, frequented by more than 800,000 people annually.

Photo by Bob Boyer, Courtesy of River Valley Partners, Inc.

Clever bypasses and serpentine access ramps like this one (lit at night) were devised to overcome seemingly insurmountable features, such as cliffs and highways.

Appalachian National Scenic Trail

Maine, New Hampshire, Vermont,
Massachusetts, Connecticut, New York,
New Jersey, Pennsylvania, Maryland,
West Virginia, Virginia, Tennessee,
North Carolina, and Georgia

A hiker takes a break by Catfish Pond Gap, in New Jersey.

Photo by Gary W. Szelc. Courtesy of the Appalachian Trail Conference.

With its combination of eight national forests, two national parks, and several state preserves, the Appalachian Trail has become a vast central park for the eastern seaboard, one of the most densely inhabited regions in the world. Riding the crest of the Appalachian mountains for more than 2,000 miles, the Trail is a long thin strip of public land extending from Georgia to Maine. It offers endless opportunities for recreation and adventure to the more than 150 million people who live within a day's drive.

But a haven for day-trippers and weekend excursionists is not what Benton MacKaye, the Harvard social reformist who envisioned the trail in 1921, had in mind. He meant the Trail to be a catalyst for the development of small rural

Completed between 1921 and 1937, the Appalachian Trail meanders for more than two thousand miles across the Appalachian mountain range, from Springer Mountain, in northern Georgia, to Mount Katahdin, in central Maine.

A Thin Green Line

Harvard social reformist Benton MacKaye viewed the American landscape as a battleground on which the forces of a monolithic metropolitan culture were locked in conflict with local rural and indigenous cultures. He saw a "worldwide standardized civilization formed around modern industry and commerce" that was threatening to swallow up America's "quiltwork of varied cultures, each with its own environment and regional setting." The Appalachian Trail, as he envisioned it, would stop the advance of the metropolitan culture and nourish a resurgence of rural living.

Several other social reformists of the time shared MacKaye's views and helped him turn his vision of the Trail into reality. Prominent among them were Clarence Stein and Louis Mumford, who, as members of the Regional Planning Association of America, facilitated the first meeting of what later became the Appalachian Trail Conference. According to MacKaye, "The creation of the Conference was one of two pivotal events in the history of the Trail; the second was the signing of the National Trails System Act in 1968. The first provided a parent organization for clubs whose members work at maintaining the trail; the second provided federal protection for it."

communities along its path, offering living conditions drastically different from those of large cities; it was meant to be a dam to contain and, ultimately, halt the spread of urbanization. Seventy-five years later, however, the region's cities have grown beyond MacKaye's worst imaginings. Meant to inspire a return to a rural way of life, the Trail has instead became a place that makes urban life more feasible. ∎

Little Rock Knob, on the North Carolina and Tennessee border.

Union Square Market

Manhattan, New York

Union Square Market, the showcase of the Greenmarket Farmers' Market system, is the only link most residents of Manhattan have with the surrounding farmlands of Long Island, upstate New York, and New Jersey. It helps New Yorkers establish mutually nourishing relationships with the region's farmers in which they obtain better, fresher produce while also helping to strengthen local agriculture. The Market presents a tangible image of an interdependent relationship—one that the supermarket chains and interstate food trucking interests have almost completely erased—between the city and region.

There are no figures on how many acres of land the Market supports; whatever the number, it helps many farmers in the region remain productive and protects farms close to the city from urban development. Some two hundred farmers sell their produce at 19 different sites around New York City, generating approximately $18 million dollars in annual sales—half of which comes from Union Square.

Not only can urbanites who shop at the Union Square farmers' market buy the best fruits and vegetables available in the city, they can also discuss produce quality with the growers and share food tips—sometimes with the city's best-known chefs, who are the market's early morning customers.

Like most public markets, the Union Square greenmarket is really more of an event than a place. Four days a week this empty lot at the intersection of three subway lines fills up with people, colors, and aromas. It becomes an arena in which local politicians greet their constituents, community and special interest groups disseminate information, local musicians perform, and neighbors from all corners of the region meet. ■

A Market of a Different Sort

Although it has no permanent physical structure, the Market has had a positive impact on Union Square. A few years ago, the area was a drug trafficker's market, but today it is cleaner and safer than it has been for decades; some of the city's best restaurants and shops have opened nearby, new apartment towers have been built, and many of the old manufacturing lofts have been transformed into residences and small businesses. The Market has played a pivotal role in the renaissance of Union Square by drawing New Yorkers determined to get fresh fruits and vegetables. Their consistent presence during the week has displaced the heavy drug trade and helped make the area ripe for redevelopment.

The Greenmarket Program

The farmers' market on Union Square was opened in 1977 by architect Barry Benepe, founder of the Greenmarket Farmers' Market program and a consultant to the Council on the Environment of New York. Concerned about the poor quality of produce available in the city and about the extinction of nearby farms, he opened the first market in 1976 with a group of nine farmers. Since then, he has started 33 markets on 23 sites, the largest of which is at Union Square. The Council on the Environment manages the greenmarkets by charging for the stands and collecting five percent of the farmers' gross. Although the group works through the Mayor's office, it is a private, nonprofit organization, directed by Benepe.

The market transforms a drab, empty space in Union Square into a brilliantly colored set that changes with the season: fall squash replaces summer tomatoes; spring greens replace winter roots.

Pleasurable Rides

As the human and physical costs associated with commuting and urban sprawl mount, public transportation is making a comeback: light rail and streetcars have been introduced in many cities, including San Diego, Portland, and Toronto; the use of ferries is expanding in Seattle, Boston, and New York. Large metropolitan areas around the country are rediscovering how transportation can be a powerful place maker, by influencing the form of city life with well-designed routes, vehicles, and terminals.

The definition of a public place can be expanded to include New Orleans' St. Charles Avenue Streetcars—spirited public-meeting rooms that traverse the city's neighborhoods—and the San Francisco Bay ferries, with their magnificent commute. The Brooklyn Bridge Walkway celebrates the pleasures of walking, the Blue Ridge Parkway the pleasures of driving. Pioneer Courthouse Square, in Portland, Oregon, and Union Station, in Los Angeles, demonstrate transportation's ability to recreate urban environments. ∎

St. Charles Avenue Streetcars

New Orleans, Louisiana

Although they are, quite literally, on the move, the St. Charles Avenue streetcars do what all great public places should do—provide a congenial setting where people can meet. The streetcars service a wide mix of residents from the diverse neighborhoods in their six-mile path. Neighbors and friends strike up informal conversations, and tourists get a rare opportunity to share an intimate moment with locals.

The glossy wood trim and brass detailing of the period cars, the slow wobbly ride, and the rhythmic clatter (not to mention the absence of gasoline fumes) all contribute to the agreeable atmosphere. The cars skim the grassy median, sometimes at speeds barely faster than a walk, offering passengers ample time to take in the flowering shrubs, majestic trees, and stately homes on either side of the street. Yet the streetcars are not simply nostalgic souvenirs of the past. For those who live or work along the avenue, they are the most convenient way to get around.

Contrary to the belief that properties situated on transit corridors are inherently unattractive, St. Charles Avenue is one of New Orleans' most desirable locations; real estate values are consistently higher than they are for comparable buildings located just a block away. It shouldn't be surprising, though: the St. Charles median strip is planted with flowering camellia and azalea bushes, and live oaks canopy most of the boulevard, lending it a serene, almost rural, character. The streetcars' green path weaves together the Uptown Neighborhoods, one of New Orleans' most diverse

The six-mile, one-way ride costs a dollar and takes nearly an hour to complete from end to end. Noisy and hot in summer and drafty in winter, the cars are elegantly appointed and provide a leisurely commute.

"To live on St. Charles Avenue, with a view of the neutral ground and brief glimpses of the ambling streetcar, is considered the most significant amenity of New Orleans residential property. This is in stark contrast to most places, where no one wants to live directly on a transit line—they want its convenience, but not its presence." Richard Sexton, from his letter of nomination.

A Venerable Commute

The St. Charles Avenue streetcar line, which began service in 1835, is one of the country's oldest trolley systems; it extends the length of St. Charles Avenue, following the curve of the Mississippi River. At one time, New Orleans was served by as many as a dozen streetcar lines, including the Desire line—immortalized by Tennessee Williams—which traveled down Bourbon Street and out to Desire Street. In 1840, the original horse- and mule-drawn cars were replaced by steam locomotives, then by electric cars, in 1893. Today, 35 wood-trimmed streetcars, purchased in 1923 and listed on the National Register, are in service.

residential areas, and gives them added character. Walkers and joggers, who use the median as a park, are as much a presence as the streetcars are. And during Mardi Gras, people from all over the world camp out on the island hours before the parade begins, to secure a prime viewing spot.

The St. Charles Avenue line has inspired a return to streetcars not only as appropriate vehicles for moving people around downtown areas but also for commuting. Whether in their traditional one-car design or in the modern multiple-car, light-rail format, streetcars offer a relaxing substitute to private automobiles. They are efficient and environmental, and their festive presence contributes to, rather than detracts from, the quality of street life. After 160 years in operation, the St. Charles Avenue streetcars are leading the way to a more humane form of commuting with old-fashioned grace. ■

Horses and mules were used to pull the streetcars until they were replaced by steam locomotives in 1840. The overhead electric wire system that exists today was introduced in 1893.

San Francisco Bay Ferries

San Francisco, California

"The ferries are one of America's most memorable commutes. Brisk winds and spectacular views define this 30-minute trip. You are free to socialize on deck, or there is a bar serving drinks inside (more notable for the ride home in the evening)." Richard Sexton, from his letter of nomination.

One of the most efficient links in the region's public transportation system, the San Francisco Bay ferries place the commuter in the center of one of the country's most beautiful landscapes, replacing the isolation and irritation of travel by car with a pleasant trip across the water. The ferries transform the bay into a watery esplanade that connects distant shores and provides a public meeting place for the nearly eight thousand people who use them each day.

Although it seems low compared with the total Bay Area commuting population, the number of ferry users continues to grow as the city's worsening traffic makes the efficiency and comfort of the ferries more desirable (a small revenge on the automobile, which hastened the ferries' demise sixty years ago, when the Golden Gate and Bay bridges opened).

From their breezy decks the ferries also offer

In the morning the mood is pensive: people read their newspapers, take catnaps, plan their daily schedules; in the afternoon, occasional entertainment creates a festive atmosphere.

White Arks

The completion of San Francisco's Union Ferry Depot, in 1903, marked the peak of a golden era in ferry travel. Luxuriously appointed ferries nicknamed "white arks" carried up to twenty-five hundred passengers and offered the services of restaurants, bars, newsstands, shoeshine booths, and private lounges for ladies. More than 50 million people passed through the depot's turnstiles each year, making it one of the busiest passenger terminals in the world. The opening of both the San Francisco-Oakland Bay Bridge, in 1936, and the Golden Gate Bridge, in 1937, however, spelled the end of the great ferry fleets. By the early 1940s, virtually all commercial service had ceased, and it was not until 1969 that it was resumed, on a modest basis.

direct and dramatic views of the Bay, access to the open water, and a chance to put the San Francisco Bay, with its natural and man-made landmarks, into grand perspective. Commuters are treated to spectacular views that change as the sun rises and sets, while they relax in the company of fellow-travelers. ∎

The vessels of the Golden Gate and Red & White ferry companies connect San Francisco's Ferry Building with terminals in Sausalito, Tiburon, Larkspur, Vallejo, and Oakland. The ferries' importance to Bay Area residents becomes clear every time a natural disaster forces the closing of one of the bridges. In 1982, when mud slides shut down the Golden Gate Bridge, the ferries became the only link between Marin County and San Francisco.

Brooklyn Bridge Promenade

Brooklyn, New York

John Roebling, the designer of the Brooklyn Bridge, conceived the Promenade as a place to celebrate the pleasures of walking, thus turning one of the 19th century's most brilliant pieces of engineering into an exalted urban experience that is enjoyed by thousands of New Yorkers.

Nowhere else in the city is the pedestrian treated with such respect. Eighteen feet above the roadway of the Bridge, the stroller (along with the jogger, cyclist, and rollerblader) is king. While the walkways of most bridges are dominated by cars and force pedestrians onto narrow sidewalks, the Brooklyn Bridge Promenade is wide and raised above the traffic, where walkers and bench-sitters, unlike drivers, can take in the views of the East River and the Manhattan skyline undistracted.

In many ways, the conception of the Promenade stemmed from a civic desire—similar to the concerns

that led to the creation of Central Park and Prospect Park fifty years earlier—to provide relief from the dehumanizing aspects of living in the city. In that regard, the Brooklyn Bridge Promenade was an instant success: from midnight until dawn on inauguration day, 150,000 people walked across the bridge for the sheer pleasure of it. It has since become one of the most cherished public places in the city, an icon celebrated in books and poetry, on stage and in the movies, but mostly in the lives of the ordinary citizens who use it. ■

A Fine Bridge For Walking

For several days during the last major public-transportation strike in New York City, in the mid-eighties, the Brooklyn Bridge Promenade became the only way to cross the river from Brooklyn to Manhattan. Workers by the thousands walked the bridge twice a day, following in the footsteps of Brooklynites before them, who began using the bridge in May of 1883 as a cost-free alternative to the ferry. Within five years of the bridge's opening, 30 million people a year were shuttling across on trains, leaving the Promenade the province of leisure walkers.

"To be on the promenade of the Brooklyn Bridge on a fine day, about halfway between the two towers, looking over the harbor and the city skyline, was to be at one of the two or three most soul-stirring spots in America, like standing at the rim of the Grand Canyon."
—David G. McCullough, *The Great Bridge,* New York, 1972

Union Station

Los Angeles, California

Familiar from dozens of movies and Raymond Chandler novels, the Art Deco interiors of Union Station have become synonymous with the romance and nostalgia of transcontinental train travel. The terminal, completed in 1939, was the last of the great railroad stations built in the United States.

A beloved Los Angeles landmark, Union Station was nearly deserted until a few years ago. Today, as the centerpiece of both a private redevelopment project—the Gateway at Union Station—and a new regional commuter rail network, it is about to become one of the busiest passenger terminals in the country, a transformation that will radically restructure downtown Los Angeles and turn the heart of the city into a clean and efficient public-transportation hub.

The Gateway development, a 68-acre commercial and residential complex, will wrap Union Station in seven million square feet of new building space for offices, shops, convention and cultural facilities, hotels, and residences, all within a few blocks of the Station, reshaping the area into a new business and activity center for the region.

Unlike most other major railroad terminals, Union Station was designed from the beginning to link rail with the automobile. As a result, it was built as a free-standing building with convenient access roads and ample parking.

Mass Transit Returns to Los Angeles

In an ironic twist, the Los Angeles region is reconstructing —at an estimated cost of $140 billion—the public transportation system it demolished in 1938, just as Union Station was being erected. Though only a fraction of the original 1,600-mile system is being rebuilt, by the year 2004 Union Station is expected to become the country's second-largest commuter terminal, the hub of a regional mass-transit system that will include subways, trolleys, rail, light rail, and buses. The number the Station serves is expected to climb from 35,000 to 100,000 passengers a day within the next two years.

The massive scale of the Gateway development, however, raises important questions about the ultimate fate of Union Station. In architect renderings of the way the development might look once it is completed, the terminal is all but hidden by the tall buildings clustered around it. We hope that as final plans take shape, this Los Angeles landmark will remain a strong visual presence instead of becoming one more illustrious victim—and symbol—of the increased privatization of our public realm. ∎

An artist's rendering of the proposed development, the Gateway at Union Station, shows the terminal's front facade hidden behind new buildings.

Pioneer Courthouse Square

Portland, Oregon

Pioneer Courthouse Square is a rare example of a successful modern downtown plaza. One reason it works so well is that Portland residents, having fought and paid for it, own it. (In fact, it is paved with bricks bearing the names of the thousands who contributed to its construction.) Another is that an enlightened transportation policy has made it the main terminal of a regional light-rail system that brings thousands of passengers to work every day.

Pioneer Courthouse Square, a multilevel, brick-paved urban place, is the design of Portland architect Willard K. Martin, who also deserves a great deal of credit for sparking the interest and support of the community.

Before the Square was built, this expensive piece of downtown real estate had, inexplicably, been occupied by a dingy multistory parking garage. It took years of community pressure and a massive citizen-led campaign to convince elected officials and local businessmen that the site could be put to better use. Residents helped select the design, raised the $1.6 million required to implement it, and applied the necessary pressure to get the project completed when it faltered.

Two years after the Square's opening, the second light-rail system in the country was introduced in Portland. Although it turned out to be a less than successful experiment in Buffalo, New York, light rail not only worked in Portland, it also added to the Square's popularity. About 43 percent of the 90,000 downtown workers use mass transit, 8,000 board or disembark at the Courthouse Square stop daily.

To the surprise of many, the light rail carries more people on Saturday than on any other day of the week, indicating that downtown is thriving well

More than 300 events take place annually in the square's amphitheater; at such times, spectators fill every available seat and spill over to the plaza below.

beyond the nine-to-five business cycle, thanks to Pioneer Square and the rail system. This unexpected development has played a very large part in restoring downtown Portland as the region's social and economic center. ■

Portland's residents have been enthusiastic supporters of the light-rail system serving Pioneer Square. Since the first line opened ten years ago, they have approved extensions of the system twice—by 73 percent in 1990 and by 65 percent in 1994. As a result, the current east-west line has been extended by 12 miles, and a new north-south line will soon be under construction.

A Roundabout Route to a Square

The events that led to the building of Pioneer Courthouse Square offer insights into the often messy way we make decisions in our cities.

In 1952, a two-story parking garage was built on the site where the grand Portland Hotel had stood for more than sixty years. Ten years later, a part-time architect for the city proposed replacing the garage with a public square with parking underneath, but the city ignored the idea and instead decided to expand the garage in 1969. After heated opposition at several public hearings, however, Portland's Planning Commission rejected the plan.

Then, in 1972, the Downtown Plan for Portland designated the block for future use as a square. The city purchased the land in 1979 and the next year held an international competition to select a design for the square. A citizen jury chose the scheme of a local team of architects headed by Willard K. Martin. Although a new mayor and the Downtown Business Association for Portland Progress brought all plans to a halt, a grass-roots group called the Friends of Pioneer Square took up fund-raising for the project. They raised the $1.6 million needed by selling the future square's benches, trees, and lights, plus more than 60,000 bricks. The parking garage was finally demolished, and in 1984, nine thousand citizens attended the opening celebrations of their own Pioneer Courthouse Square.

Blue Ridge Parkway

Virginia and North Carolina

A Good Excuse for a Road

A small portion of the Blue Ridge Parkway was built before World War I with the intent of making the scenic splendor of the Blue Ridge Mountains accessible to a new motoring public. The project languished, however, until the Depression, when talk of federal park-to-park highways revived interest in finishing the Parkway, partially because of the jobs it would create. The Parkway's construction was authorized under the directives of the National Industrial Recovery Act of 1933 (a program designed to put people back to work). Construction began in 1935. A year later, the Blue Ridge Parkway became part of the National Park System.

The Blue Ridge Parkway is a narrow, curvy, two-lane highway with 45-mile-per-hour speed limit—not the kind of road that someone in a rush would choose to take. It was clearly designed for leisure, which is what attracts the estimated 22 million passengers who use it each year. Free of convenience stores, gas stations, and billboards, the landscape along the road seems as untouched and as beautiful as the two national parks it connects.

Although this book focuses on pedestrians and public transportation, we've included the Blue Ridge Parkway because we wanted to acknowledge the undeniable role of the automobile in our society and to applaud a pleasurable and civilized use of it. The Parkway is a rare road that effectively turns driving into a pleasant pursuit. ■

Courtesy of National Park Service.

The Blue Ridge Parkway follows the spine of the Southern Appalachians for 469 miles and connects two national parks: Shenandoah National Park, in Virginia, and the Great Smoky Mountains National Park, on the North Carolina-Tennessee border.

Courtesy of Asheville/Buncombe Co., NC Tourism Development Authority.

"The Blue Ridge Parkway teaches us some superb lessons that we have chosen to ignore. Beauty and the quality of the driving experience have not been sacrificed for the sake of speed. While most roads tend to get bigger and commercialized, the Parkway steadfastly remains two-lane and maintains a maximum speed of 45 miles per hour. These are lessons we should apply nationwide."

From the panel discussion.

A jogger enjoys the Blue Ridge Parkway near Ashville, N.C.

Small Towns

The seven places included here are all survivors, not only of the vicissitudes of time, but of tourism, one of the most potentially disruptive forces facing towns of particular historical, architectural, and cultural significance. Through cycles of economic prosperity and decline, they have managed to reinvent themselves without losing their integrity as communities.

By capitalizing on its history, Charleston, South Carolina, has taken advantage of tourism without compromising quality of life. The island town of Nantucket, Massachusetts, under constant attack from developers, is an exceptional example of historic preservation and natural conservation. New Harmony, Indiana, has created a niche for itself in convention tourism, wooing high-level conferences to its time-capsule charms in the Indiana cornfields. Portsmouth, New Hampshire, and Greenwich, New York, are typical small American towns that are atypical in having escaped the urban renewal that has destroyed so many others like them. The Native American pueblos of Acoma and Taos, both in New Mexico, have preserved their unique form and culture for hundreds of years. ∎

Wooden ladders at Acoma Pueblo, in New Mexico

Four Towns

Nantucket, Massachusetts
New Harmony, Indiana
Portsmouth, New Hampshire
Greenwich, New York

Nantucket, New Harmony, Portsmouth, and the village of Greenwich are classic examples of the traditional American small town, a complex and compact world where a friendly, laid-back lifestyle prevails, and where most necessities are still within a short walk of people's homes.

Situated in splendid natural settings undisturbed by suburban and commercial growth, all four towns have a wealth of well-kept parks and squares, interesting buildings, beautiful residential streets, old trees, carefully landscaped yards, and prosperous main streets. Because of protracted economic decline, however, progress bypassed them, sparing them the ravages characteristic of urban development of the past fifty years—namely the wholesale demolition of historic structures and the disintegration of original town plans. Once the towns were able to restore their historic districts, they became the focus of outside attention that attracted tourists and new residents.

Along with tourism and gentrification, however, have come new problems. The population of Nantucket, a chic resort community with most of its historic architecture intact, swells in summer from 7,000 to 45,000—a development that profits the town while straining its resources. Real-estate values

In 1814, a group of German millennialists led by George Rapp founded New Harmony, where they shared labor and property while awaiting the Second Coming. Rapp sold the town in 1824 to the wealthy industrialist Robert Owen, whose secular experiment in communal living lasted two years.

Courtesy of the Nantucket Historical Association.

Nantucket's plain, almost severe, architecture dates from its days as a 19th-century whaling center; very few of the buildings from this era have been lost.

fueling new construction and exerting pressure on the island's limited supply of land. Although residents stand to benefit handsomely from this growth, they are fighting it in the interest of protecting the island's fragile environment. So far, they have managed to stave off construction that does not conform with the island's architectural and natural character.

Some 40,000 people a year visit the tiny town of New Harmony, Indiana, built in the 1800s by two different utopian movements. Now a living museum, New Harmony was resurrected by several philanthropic institutions, which restored, rebuilt, and resited historic structures (particularly those related to the original settlements), and meticulously reconstructed the town plan. They also helped recruit well-known contemporary architects to build facilities that would interpret New Harmony's intellectual and religious past. In addition to convention facilities and hotels, these include Philip Johnson's Roofless

Stewards of History

Nantucket, with its simple, almost severe, Quaker-inspired architecture and pristine natural environment, is one of the most impressive historic districts in the country. Once a wealthy 19th-century whaling town, the island is now besieged by developers and has some of the country's strictest building controls.

The Historic District Commission, which began the preservation of the town of Nantucket in 1956, is responsible for the way Nantucket looks today. Under its jurisdiction more than eight hundred buildings—ranging from the stately homes of the rich to the humble homes of shopkeepers, craftsmen, and schoolteachers—have been restored.

The Commission has processed some 26,000 applications seeking approval on everything from the color of a building's trim to the construction of Nashaquisset, a new subdivision. Although the Commission requires that all new buildings conform with the architectural vernacular, the diverse and idiosyncratic styles of the island's buildings defy monotony.

Courtesy of Historic New Harmony.

New Harmony's history is re-enacted in such scenes as this candle-dipping, held in front of a replica of an early Harmonist cabin.

Courtesy of Historic New Harmony.

Citizens and visitors enjoy a concert on the green, at the corner of Church and Main streets. To its credit, New Harmony has not sacrificed its identity as a community by becoming a period theme park.

Church (1960) and Richard Meier's Athenaeum (1979). Tourism here is a well-choreographed business: the town attracts small, high-level political and scientific conferences (in keeping with the unusual number of pioneering scientists and educators who have called New Harmony home), as well as visitors who want to experience a genuine piece of Americana.

Portsmouth and Greenwich benefit from tourism in a different way. Although neither is in itself a destination, both are located in major tourist markets—Portsmouth in New England, and Greenwich in New York's Capital-Saratoga Region—and both enjoy a steady stream of visitors who help to support an unusual number of amenities. (Portsmouth, for example, with a population of only 24,000, has nearly a hundred restaurants.) Their proximity to large metropolitan areas is also a draw for people seeking the tranquillity and high quality of small-town life.

The question now is whether these four towns can continue to withstand the pressures attendant upon their prosperity. The answer is probably yes—provided that each finds the strength to establish strict controls on growth, whether caused by

Courtesy of Prescott Park Arts Festival.

Portsmouth, which has no less than nine theater companies, fifteen art galleries, three recording studios, a ballet company, a public amphitheater, and 96 restaurants, enjoys a cultural vitality remarkable for a town of its size. At the annual Prescott Park Arts Festival, Marian Marangelli performed "Rocky Hampshire and the Drydocks."

Photo by Daniel T. Seginak.

With just one traffic light and no traffic to speak of, the village of Greenwich, New York, is exceptional for having escaped such modern intrusions as commercial strips and malls. Its lively Main Street thrives for lack of direct competition from national chains. The town's one shopping plaza—a supermarket and perhaps a dozen stores—is located well away from downtown.

gentrification or tourism. When these towns were created, it was commonly believed that the act of building would increase the town's beauty and common good, but that's not the case today. What cities and small towns once achieved on a voluntary basis must now be implemented through tough laws and regulations. ■

Stewards of Nature

The Nantucket Conservation Foundation works parallel to the Historic District Commission, insuring that the process of renewal includes all the elements that promote quality of life, chief among them being the conservation of 25 percent of the island's natural habitat. In 1983, Nantucket passed a controversial land-preservation ordinance requiring new developments to pay a two-percent transfer fee on all real-estate transactions. The funds are used by the Foundation to acquire land—over 700 acres have been purchased and protected in this way.

Photo by Daniel T. Seginak.

Greenwich's neighborhoods of well-preserved homes date from the turn of the century.

Charleston

South Carolina

Charleston's Old and Historic District—the country's first designated historic district—contains many 18th- and 19th-century mansions built in the distinctive Charleston style. All but 50 of the 572 landmarks listed in a 1941 architectural survey conducted by the city still stand.

Much of Charleston's beauty can be found in the details.

Charleston is, possibly, the most beautiful small city in the country—not just for its sheer physical elegance but for its tremendous diversity and contradictions. Charleston's citizens and leaders have consistently solved complex problems through dialogue and democracy. Working hand in hand to build a modern, well-functioning community without damaging or compromising their inheritance, they have balanced preservation with redevelopment, used tourism to revive the city without overwhelming it, and created a climate in which residents and tourists comfortably coexist.

Charleston's achievement is due not to any single major project but to many small ones: a height-restriction ordinance, which has preserved the striking skyline of church spires and trees; an ordinance limiting hotel construction, even in commercially zoned areas; an ordinance drastically limiting tour-bus routes, which keeps the streets of the historic areas serene; and aggressive programs to increase home ownership in the historic district, which have enabled longtime low- and middle-income residents to buy and restore deteriorating houses, in turn adding to the area's racial and economic diversity. The list goes on, but mandated restrictions, strategic thinking in tourism development, and progressive housing policies are only half of the story.

The other half comes from the everyday citizens, in wealthy and poor areas alike, who lavish great care on their properties and, by extension, on their city. Their contributions—a beautifully planted front yard, a fine stone pathway, a wrought-iron gate left ajar so that passersby can peek at a backyard garden— enhance the sense of discovery that the city offers at every turn and add to a layering of color and texture that no single designer could conceive alone and no single entity could afford to maintain.

Foresight, a certain amount of good luck, and the alertness of leaders and citizens have transformed Charleston from a poverty-stricken town, "too poor to

Lessons From Ansonborough

In an early case of gentrification and displacement, the renovation of Charleston's Ansonborough district set off an alarm that convinced city officials of the need to preserve community diversity. Ansonborough was the city's first suburb, colonized by wealthy merchants and planters who built mansions there beginning in the 1740s. By the time it caught the attention of the Charleston Foundation, in the 1950s, it had deteriorated into a slum. Led by Frances Edmunds, the daughter of an old Charleston family, the Foundation began restoration of the area using the nation's first revolving fund to purchase, restore, and resell homes with preservation covenants attached. The effort, an acknowledged success, greatly enlarged the boundaries of Charleston's early Old and Historic District. One of its major side effects, however, was the displacement of the neighborhood's original African-American residents. Largely in response to Ansonborough, the city launched its home-ownership program, in the late 1970s, to help low- and middle-income residents in other historic districts buy and restore their homes.

A stroll through Charleston reveals intimate details of the private lives of its citizens.

The Old City Market, a series of low, narrow, open-air sheds housing restaurants, shops, and vegetable-and-fruit vendors is popular with both tourists and residents.

paint and too proud to whitewash," into a balanced and prosperous community, one of the nation's premier historic and cultural centers. As Charleston's mayor, Joseph P. Riley, Jr., eloquently put it, "If eternal vigilance is the price of liberty, eternal vigilance is also the price of a great city." ■

Traditional crafts like basket weaving are performed at the Old City Market.

Acoma and Taos

New Mexico

We can only imagine the rich community life of the pueblo—or glimpse it in photographs, such as this early 20th-century image of the festival of San Geronimo, patron saint of Taos Pueblo, taken before visitors were excluded from important religious rituals.

To protect their traditions while taking advantage of tourism (a critical source of income), the tribal elders of Acoma and Taos have turned their villages into gated attractions. For eight hours each day tourism dominates the pueblos, but visitors' movements and opportunities for exchanges with Native American residents are limited and many basic daily tasks are put on hold when outsiders are present. Although the system frustrates visitors and makes residents, who live a kind of double life, resentful, a more accommodating solution might imperil the pueblo way of life.

It is astonishing that Acoma and Taos, two of the country's oldest continuously inhabited pueblo settlements, have remained intact in form and spirit. (Taos dates to the sixteenth century; Acoma, to 1075.) The feeling that one is visiting an archaeological site rather than a living city is

Photo by George L. Beam. Courtesy of the Museum of New Mexico.

Taos

As far back as the 1500s, when the Spanish first set eyes upon it, Taos Pueblo has existed much as we see it today. Its longevity is the result of the aggressive efforts of Taos's tribal leaders to protect their traditions. In the past, they did so through wars and rebellions; today they must fight in court—most recently to regain control of Blue Lake, a sacred site, and to stave off attempts to close down the Pueblo on the grounds of substandard living conditions. Pueblo leaders must also contend with a more subtle enemy: the seductive power of a more comfortable lifestyle. Such basic amenities as electricity, television, and telephones do not exist in the Pueblo, and, consequently, many young people have moved away. Nevertheless, Taos has succeeded in preserving its physical integrity better than any other Native American city.

Ceremonies and festivals are held in the streets and squares of the pueblos. This historic photo, taken in the 19th century, during the San Geronimo festival at Taos, captures the traditional relay race run between the north and south ends of the pueblo.

compounded by the fact that the shape of the pueblos is unlike that of other North American towns. There are no main streets, no commercial buildings, no parks, trees, sidewalks, or benches—none of the the signs that normally suggest the existence of community life. Indeed, Acoma seems to lack a central meeting place altogether, while Taos's central plaza (which connects the north and south ends of the pueblo) looks like a huge dusty parking lot—which is what it becomes during visiting hours. In the absence of the familiar landmarks of public life, the pueblos become enigmatic, conveying only the exotic and mysterious beauty of the ancient buildings.

The rich and complex way of life at Acoma and Taos is, to a great degree, communal; civic and spiritual activities overlap in ways that are totally unfamiliar to our Western culture. Though many members live outside the pueblos, particularly at Acoma, they return regularly throughout the year to participate in religious ceremonies, an important part of the life cycle. It is largely through

The three-story, terraced, stone-and-adobe dwellings of Acoma Pueblo are built in three parallel rows running east to west. Near the center they are crossed by a short, wide corridor that forms a plaza. Traditionally, the first story, originally used for storage, had no entrance except for a trapdoor in the ceiling. Ladders led from the ground to the living quarters on the second floor (as shown in this photo from 1882). The third story and the roof were reached by a set of steep external stairs.

these rituals (which have been declared off-limits to outsiders) that the tribal society has been held together and the ancient traditions have been handed down to the next generation. ▪

Sky City

Although Acoma is nearly uninhabited today—only some 20 families live there—it remains the vital spiritual center of the Keresan tribe. Built on top of a high mesa in the middle of a remote desert valley, the pueblo appears to be a natural extension of the exposed rock surface. There is no electricity or water, and until relatively recently the only route to the top was the original foot trail. A road, paid for and built by a film crew, has made access easier, but most of the Pueblo's 4,000 members prefer to live on the valley floor, near their farms, returning frequently to Acoma to participate in the annual dances and to perform private religious rituals.

An aerial view (above) shows the extraordinary location of the Acoma Pueblo, on top of a remote New Mexico mesa. Timber (below) and stone (left) are the main building materials.

Planned Communities

The three planned communities presented here are examples of flourishing places designed (or redesigned) according to nearly forgotten traditional town-planning principles. Self-contained and walkable, with clearly defined public and private domains, they demonstrate the superior ability of such plans to foster a strong sense of community pride.

Yorkship Village, built by the federal government toward the end of World War I, has withstood the test of time, maintaining strong property values and a healthy appearance while the neighborhoods surrounding it have deteriorated. Seaside, a privately developed resort town and a relative newcomer at age fifteen, has achieved a formidable economic success despite predictions to the contrary. Perhaps most dramatic is Diggs Town, a typical public-housing wasteland that has been transformed into an integrated Norfolk neighborhood and is now experiencing a resurgence as a community. ■

Diggs Town, Norfolk, Virginia.

Courtesy of UDA Architects.

Yorkship Village

Camden, New Jersey

The many private gardens in Yorkship helped secure the town's inclusion, in 1974, on the National Register of Historic Places.

Yorkship Village, recently rechristened Fairview, was the country's first planned working-class community. Built by the federal government to house the wartime workers of a nearby shipyard, it has thrived since its completion, in 1918, even as the areas around it have slipped into a precipitous decline. Its solid town plan has favored the evolution of a tightly knit community: many of the houses—sturdy brick Colonial residences—are still occupied by their original tenants, who have altered their homes in hundreds of different ways over time rather than move elsewhere. As a result, a pleasant visual anarchy reigns, giving Yorkship a comfortable, well-adapted look.

The curvilinear streets of this small, self-contained village (Yorkship has its own school, library, post office, market, and churches) radiate outward in a weblike pattern from Yorkship Square, the town's social center. The tallest buildings enclose the square, turning it into a public room. Buildings located at the corners of major intersections have unusually large front yards that create miniature squares, while the backyards of homes open onto small common playgrounds (which are, unfortunately, now used mostly for parking) and onto a system of busy pedestrian alleyways. Tall trees, low fences, and short, narrow streets—often barely the width of two cars—allow children to play freely and neighbors to keep an eye on things.

While Yorkship has thus far enjoyed a stable population, its makeup has begun to change as older people leave and younger residents—many with jobs in Camden or Philadelphia—move in. These new inhabitants tend not to shop on the town square or send their children to the village school. They treat Yorkship more like a suburb or a dormitory community than like the self-sufficient town it was designed to be. Consequently, it is losing its extraordinary cohesiveness and vitality despite its admirable plan. ∎

Kids are kings of the streets in Yorkship.

The various picket-fence designs reflect the personal tastes of Yorkship's homeowners.

The Wartime Effort

America's entry into the war in Europe, in the spring of 1917, thrust the federal government into the role of town builder. Since the war seemed likely to continue for years, the American Institute of Architects recommended that the government build well-planned, landscaped villages for its workers rather than impermanent barracks. The best architects and planners of the time were hired for the effort, and within four months they constructed more than 33,000 housing units—nearly a fifth of all the housing built in the United States in 1918.

Yorkship, designed by Electus Darwin Litchfield and built on an irregular 225-acre tract outside Camden, New Jersey, was the first village to be completed. Its tenants moved in just a month after the Armistice was signed, and when the government no longer needed the houses it auctioned them, in 1921. The original tenants, who were allowed to match any bid, purchased a majority of the properties—which doubled in value in just three years.

In an article published soon after Yorkship's completion, the Journal of the American Institute of Architects praised the town: "If [Yorkship] indicates the kind of government housing that is to follow, we may all rejoice." Unfortunately, the performance has yet to be repeated.

Diggs Town

Norfolk, Virginia

During meetings with architects, residents recalled the fences that once surrounded their front yards. These were reintroduced, along with backyard patios equipped with "privacy fences" and traditional front-yard porches for outdoor living.

The Diggs Town housing project was once a dangerous, decaying, 30-acre island of impenetrable superblocks where gunshots rang out in the night. Today, thanks to a unique collaboration between architects and tenants, it has become a genuine neighborhood, with lovingly tended yards and flower gardens, safe, well-traveled streets, and a burgeoning sense of community.

Architects began the redesign by opening up the project to the surrounding neighborhoods and transforming it into a series of small villages. New streets and paths have given it the texture of a normal neighborhood in which each unit faces a street and has its own address and front yard. Picket fences help define private and public areas, and traditional porches allow tenants to talk with neighbors while keeping an eye on the street. Drug dealers, finding little privacy in the narrow streets, have gone elsewhere, and crime and violence have decreased. And now that they are in charge of the space in front of their homes, residents have begun to care for their properties and take pride in them.

While no one believes that the physical changes in Diggs Town have solved all of its problems (sixty-five percent of the 4,000 tenants live below the poverty line), the newly energized community has been liberated from the stigma attached to public housing. ∎

Diggs Town housing units, before and after they were redesigned. Like most of the subsidized housing projects built in the early 1950s, Diggs Town, the first such project built under the Housing Act of 1949, was a failure. Its anonymous, barracks-like brick buildings created an institutional environment devoid of a sense of security or community, with no demarcation of public and private areas.

Building Community

Faced with the physical decay and social collapse of Diggs Town, the Norfolk Redevelopment and Housing Authority made two good decisions: to retrofit rather than simply bulldoze the site (thus sparing residents from displacement) and to bring residents together with the Pittsburgh-based design firm of UDA Architects. In a series of public meetings, tenants and architects developed the idea of turning the housing project into a real neighborhood. The project, which began in 1989, was completed in 1994.

Motivated by their success, residents have enacted new educational and social programs. An early-childhood center, part of the Norfolk public school system, now provides educational services for 180 area three-year-olds, as well as adult classes in child care. Also in the works are a monthly newsletter, tutoring and mentoring programs for children and young people, and a program to help welfare recipients. This is just the beginning: "The glass wall around Diggs Town has just begun to be shattered," says one resident. Now, adds another, the community needs to focus on jobs, because "jobs are a way of restoring hope, and the thing that is still missing is hope."

Seaside

Florida

A concert on Seaside's village green. In the background are two public buildings—the stucco-clad administration building and the corrugated-metal market and meeting hall—that comprise the town's commercial core.

Seaside, perhaps the most controversial planned community of the last fifteen years, has been discussed, documented, applauded, berated, and imitated by architects and planners around the country. Located on 80 acres of the Florida Panhandle, 40 miles west of Panama City, Seaside owes part of its fame to its developer and designers, who planned the town according to building principles not used for decades, which went against the grain of accepted practices. Whereas most new developments today are exclusive and private, for instance, they made Seaside open and accessible to the public. And they instituted rigorous building restrictions, rejecting the commonly held belief that developments that impose too many limitations don't sell well.

In an age in which the public domain of so many new communities is reserved exclusively for residents, Seaside makes a statement. Anyone driving the two-lane highway 30-A, which skirts the

Public access to the beach is marked by individually designed gazebos located at the ends of major residential streets.

The Seaside Building Codes

Seaside's success shows that buyers are willing to put up with restrictions if they are fairly administered and if their objective is to protect the community's quality and livability.

The town's Urban Code and its Building Code, which contain the essence of the plan, represent the most admired and criticized aspects of this project. On the one hand, they are applauded for providing the town with visual coherence and for protecting the quality of the street life; on the other, they are criticized (mostly by architects) for limiting individual creativity.

The Urban Code is a simple, one-page document listing permissible building types and codifying how buildings must relate to each other and to the street. It dictates the use of picket fences, porches, yards, outbuildings (granny flats), and towers (built to give homes a view of the Gulf). The Building Code mandates materials, fixtures, roof pitches, and exterior lighting. Together, they bring the plan to life in visual, three-dimensional detail.

Gulf of Mexico, can stop at the village square, park the car, and stroll through town. Seaside's inviting streets are framed by buildings of uniform height. Low picket fences, porches, narrow mid-block passageways, and public gazebos located at major intersections bring residents and visitors together, but the public and private are unequivocally defined, and the boundary lines are seldom violated.

Seaside is a distinctive presence on the Florida coast, reminiscent of the towns created by John Nolen, the father of American town planning; its orderly layout particularly resembles Nolen's plans for Kingsport, Tennessee, and Mariemont, Ohio, which he designed in 1917 and 1923, respectively. Seaside's clear spatial hierarchy—from the very public central civic square, on which commercial activities and buildings are concentrated, to the private residential streets—follows a traditional civic order present in these and such older cities as Charleston, Nantucket, and Santa Fe but conspicuously absent from most modern developments.

Seaside's controversial town plan has not stopped it from achieving an unqualified economic success. However, high property values (the average annual appreciation on lot and house resales is thirty percent) have unfortunately rendered small-scale building at Seaside unfeasible. Some of the early, more modest, idiosyncratic cottages (which contribute so much to the town's charm), if built today, would cost less than the lots they stand on. As a result, only large, costly homes are now being contructed and the overall variety of building types has diminished. Success has also attracted tourism, which has turned Seaside into more of a hotel resort—in which year-around population is low and many houses are rented to short-term visitors—than a town.

Whatever one may think of Seaside, it will not be a town in the full sense of the word until it gains a stable, full-time population that can support local businesses and elect a town government. ■

Civic landmarks, such as the Tupelo Street Pavilion, create small, secluded public settings at the intersections of major streets.

Visitors and residents encounter each other unexpectedly on the extensive system of footpaths and alleys that winds through Seaside.

"This is an age in which we are witnessing the increased privatization of the public realm, and what Seaside represents is an effort to make public the private realm, and that is exactly the opposite of what we see going on everywhere else in this country."

From the panel discussion

Seaside's rigorously detailed Building Code can translate into graceful scenes: here, palm fronds cast shadows across a butter-colored porch wall.

Endangered and
In Transition

The mention of New York's Times Square, New Orleans' French Quarter, or Brooklyn's Jacob Riis Park and Coney Island evokes powerful images, but as these places strive to redefine themselves in a time of change, they are in danger of losing the thing we prize most about them—their familiar identities.

Besieged by large-scale developments, Times Square as we know it teeters on the edge of extinction. The traditionally diverse French Quarter, though blossoming with renewal, is suffering from the predictable, safe, and homogenizing effects of tourism. Coney Island is a ghost of the extravagant resort it once was. And Jacob Riis Park has been neglected for lack of funds. ∎

For more than a hundred years, New Yorkers have been seeking diversion on the boardwalk at Coney Island.

Times Square

Manhattan, New York

Even on a cold winter's day, people crowd Times Square (the two triangular plazas—or "bow tie"—created by the intersection of Broadway and Seventh Avenue). Since 1905, when the results of the first Presidential election were beamed down from the electronic sign atop the Times Tower, the Square has been the place where New Yorkers gathered in moments of crisis and celebration.

Since the early 1980s, a sanitization campaign (which has included the redevelopment of 42nd Street) has been threatening to bury Times Square in a spurious and homogenized corporate culture and snuff out its mercurial, dynamic, often sleazy character. Focusing on tourism and business (with entertainment thrown in as a token reminder of the area's most memorable function), the redevelopment is slowly driving out not only the multitude of businesses that use the smaller, older office buildings in the district and whose workers support local shops and restaurants, but also the theater industry's eccentric support system of musical-instrument-repair shops, talent agencies, costume and prop shops, etc. Fortunately, the real-estate bust of the early 1990s has slowed the process down somewhat, giving rise to the hope that Times Square might still be rescued from a "cleaner brighter safer" fate proclaimed by the signs of the 42nd Street Development Project.

In a strategy reminiscent of 1960s urban renewal projects, the city began by demonizing Times Square. For years, it has been portrayed in the press, in movies, and on television as a crime-ridden center of the city's pornography haunts, a thoroughly blighted area embodying the worst evils of urban living. Because of this image, the area was deemed too risky to draw investors, so in the early 1980s the city offered substantial incentives, including tax write-offs and subsidies, to prospective developers, precipitating a building rush that lasted several years. Glamorous new hotels and ultra-modern office buildings sprang up along Broadway in the most substantial physical change that has ever occurred in the area.

Times Square is an exciting, fast-paced pedestrian place that surges night and day with hustlers,

Signs of the Times

Frustrated by the pervasive dullness of the Times Square redevelopment proposals, the New York Municipal Art Society, an old and powerful civic-activist organization, has sought to preserve one of the Square's most evocative elements—its huge, thousand-watt signs, the very same signs that it had

hookers, tourists, shoppers, workers, theatergoers, flashing signs, and the press of traffic. Were the Square to become a clone of Midtown's sedate business environment—which is where it is headed—this irrepressible vitality would inevitably give way to a predictable nine-to-five business rhythm. Perhaps Times Square's demons, both real and imagined, would be exorcised by such a metamorphosis, but New York—and the world—would lose one of its most charismatic urban places. ■

fought to restrain at the turn of the century.

In 1984, the Society organized a half-hour blackout of the Square, during which the Times Tower's giant television screen flashed a message to Mayor Ed Koch: "Hey, Mr. Mayor! It's dark out here. Help keep the bright lights in Times Square." As a result of the Society's crusade, a 1987 amendment was made to the Midtown district zoning laws requiring that the facades of all new buildings be decorated with an illuminated sign—an effort to restore, at least superficially, some of the character that had been destroyed.

It was perhaps a case of too little, too late. As architecture critic Ada Louise Huxtable later commented, "Never was a barn more splendidly locked after the horse was out."

Anarchy reigns in this corner of Times Square: the jumble of signs that characterizes Times Square in the popular imagination is slowly being replaced by slick, familiar, Madison Avenue graphics.

The French Quarter

New Orleans, Louisiana

New Orleans' French Quarter, or the Vieux Carre, is a diverse 100-block area encompassing the original city. Founded in 1718, it is one of the best-preserved historic districts in the country. Here quiet

Jackson Square, known as Place d'Armes to the Creoles, has become a stage for programmed activities.

"What's happening in the French Quarter is an attempt to lure and provide for visitors, who are comfortable with the ambience of the shopping mall but who are uncomfortable with real places like New Orleans or New York."

From the panel discussion.

residential Dauphine Street is just two blocks from Bourbon Street's boisterous commercialism, and a sleazy tourist trap is just around the corner from elegant Jackson Square. It is precisely this genuine mixture that has defined the Quarter's—and New Orleans'—identity and attracted visitors since the 1920s.

Unfortunately, the Quarter is slowly being upstaged by an ersatz version of itself, defined more by the needs of tourists than by the needs of residents. Its narrow, steamy, gaslit streets and 18th-century squares, once a paragon of complex urban life, have become a set for musicians, jugglers, acrobats, and other performers of dubious craft attempting to re-create a long-gone bohemian atmosphere. In Jackson Square, the picturesque center of the Quarter, the animated performances are part of a well-choreographed and regulated schedule of activities staged exclusively for tourists.

Tourism has indeed become a big business here, and tourists like places that are predictable, clean, and well organized. Though they may be drawn by the promise of adventure that the French Quarter's faintly unsavory reputation holds, it seems that instead of the unusual alligator sausages and spicy food served by local establishments, tourists want the familiar fare of the food courts and festival

Twenty years ago, the pedestrian streets of the 100-block French Quarter (the original early-18th-century city of New Orleans) had the relaxed feel of a place where real people lived.

The Cradle of Preservation

Though New Orleans became part of the United States after the Louisiana Purchase, in 1803, the Vieux Carre remained a Creole stronghold, aloof and resentful of the American newcomers. Well into the 20th century, Creole families continued to live apart in the French Quarter despite its deterioration. In the 1920s, artists and writers, attracted by the district's raw vitality, large homes, and low rents, began to settle there. Slowly the Quarter lost its déclassé status and began to acquire a romantic aura.

markets, housed in refurbished industrial buildings on the fringes of the Quarter, and they're more likely to patronize national retail establishments and large-volume T-shirt and souvenir shops than the smaller, eclectic local shops.

The Quarter raises the question of just how much we must manage our public spaces in order to accommodate tourism. Such basic needs as public safety and cleanliness must be taken care of, but cities that try to compete with the conventional environment of the micro-managed theme park risk destroying their own authenticity. ■

Out of this mix of art and fashion emerged one of the country's earliest preservation movements, the Vieux Carre Commission, established in 1925. Though it had little political clout, a Vieux Carre ordinance was passed in 1936 to protect the Quarter's distinctive character. It was not until 1941 that the legislation was interpreted by the Supreme Court of Louisiana to mean not just individual buildings in the Quarter, but the district as a whole. Several landmark decisions followed which confirmed the Commission's broad authority. The dramatic 1969 defeat of a riverfront expressway made residents aware of the irreplaceable treasures in their midst, and preservation reached a peak of prestige and power throughout the 1970s and 1980s.

The fabled French Quarter is becoming a museum perfectly preserved in all of its details.

Coney Island and Jacob Riis Park

Brooklyn, New York

Courtesy of American Media Concepts, Inc.

A s the only public bathing areas that can be reached for the price of a bus or subway token, Coney Island and Jacob Riis Park, both located in Brooklyn, are possibly the two most overused public places in New York: some fifty million people visit Coney Island each year, and five million use Riis Park. Along with Orchard Beach in the Bronx, they make the Atlantic shores accessible to those without the means to travel—a heartening fact in a metropolis the size of New York City. Both places, however, are endangered by neglect and by the huge numbers of people who patronize and, sometimes, vandalize them.

Coney Island is an amusement park, beach, boardwalk, and front yard for the dense residential neighborhoods nearby. New Yorkers go there today for the same reasons they always have: it's fun, it's cheap, and the ocean views are inspiring. Tourists are attracted by the vestiges of its glorious past—the Cyclone, the last of the original wooden roller coasters; Nathan's Famous Restaurant, renowned for its hot dogs; and the few remaining run-down arcades. On a summer's day the boardwalk is impassable and the beach is hot and crowded. Though under stress, Coney Island is at its best at such times, when thousands of people of different nationalities, speaking different languages, lie head to foot and elbow to elbow under the sun.

While Coney Island embodies New York's proverbial melting pot, Riis Park is a true microcosm of the city's ethnic patchwork of neighborhoods. Here, Brazilians, West Indians, Puerto Ricans, Costa

Though the racetracks, beach pavilions, and hotels are all gone, there are still amusements to be found at Coney Island. The rides at Astroland include the historic wood-framed Cyclone roller coaster and the Wonder Wheel.

Though built "for the people," Jacob Riis is a carefully designed park, notable for its handsome, WPA-era bathhouse.

A Park For the Poor

Jacob Riis Park is located at the western end of Brooklyn's Rockaway Peninsula, along a mile-long stretch of the Atlantic Ocean. It was named for the 19th-century social reformer and writer Jacob August Riis, who devoted his life to improving living conditions for New York's poor. During the early decades of the 20th century, he lobbied for the creation of a public oceanside park that would serve residents of the city's boroughs and be accessible by public transportation. (At the time, Coney Island was not yet linked by subway.) The park was completed in 1914, shortly after his death.

Riis Park was refurbished and enlarged during the 1930s with funding from the Works Progress Administration. An ambitious six-year restoration program conducted by the New York Parks Department's new commissioner, Robert Moses, led to the park's present form. In typical Moses style, the 1,000-car parking lot was drastically expanded to hold 7,000; the beach was divided into 14 bays separated by rock jetties and wood pilings; and the bathhouse was rebuilt to resemble the carved-stone palaces Moses built for the middle-class crowds at Long Island's Jones Beach. Today this bathhouse, one of the best examples of 1930s beachfront architecture, is listed on the National Register of Historic Places.

Ricans, Italians, nudists, surfers, and singles, among other patrons, carefully stake territories on the beach and the thin strip of parkland behind it. Samba, jazz, salsa, and the sounds of soccer games and picnic barbecues emanate from various quarters. On the boardwalk, strolling and people-watching are the main activities. With a summer peak of 150,000 visitors a day, Riis Park is quieter than Coney Island, but neglect is evident here as well—perhaps even more so, since Riis has as its backdrop a classic, still elegant 1930s bathhouse, which is in dire need of restoration.

It is hard to say what the future holds for these two places. Coney Island is periodically reinvented by entrepreneurs who hope to capitalize on its past, but these plans tend to wither as quickly as they crop up. For Riis Park, which is under the stewardship of the Gateway National Recreation Area, the future depends on federal funding—an increasingly scarce resource. Unquestionably, though, a way must be found to revive these ocean parks so that they can continue to serve the millions who go there to swim, congregate, and fill their lungs with fresh salt air. ∎

Jacob Riis Park is on the western tip of Brooklyn's Rockaway Peninsula; a little more difficult to reach than Coney Island, it is consequently less crowded.

Waterfronts

As heavy industry declines, waterfronts have become a new frontier in many cities. Long hidden by railroad tracks, highways, and large industrial areas, they have been freed for recreational development and turned into glorious public places well connected to the rest of the city.

The Venice Oceanfront Walk, in California, dates from the turn of the century, a time when recreation was becoming an important part of people's lives and waterfronts were especially popular. Some of the splendor of that era is still visible today despite the Walk's general deterioration. Ocean Drive is a seaside resort in Miami Beach, Florida, that could easily fit in on the French Riviera. Designed at the height of the Art Deco period, it is experiencing an extraordinary revival. Finally, the newly built Battery Park City Esplanade, located on the Hudson River in Lower Manhattan, is enjoying the favor of New York residents despite its daunting location within a monumental complex of corporate office buildings and luxury residences. The key to its success: art and architecture gracefully blended to create an environment full of surprise. ■

Ocean Drive, Miami.

Oceanfront Walk

Venice, California

The Oceanfront Walk, in Venice, is an original American public place that draws thousands. Rollerbladers, bodybuilders, surfers, and tourists—people of every class, race, and attitude—come together daily in an exhibitionistic spectacle that nearly blurs the line between fantasy and reality. Indeed, the energetic crowds disguise the seedy souvenir shops, the signs obscuring the original Venetian-style architecture, and the peeling murals, trampled lawns, and overflowing garbage cans.

Officials and residents recognize that the Walk has deteriorated as a result of neglect and overuse—even the expansive ocean views and vivid sunsets seem worn—but there is little agreement on what should be done about it. If cleaned up too much, the Walk would lose its appealing but precarious balance of vitality and decadence; if neglected for much longer, however, it could degrade beyond repair. ■

In his book Venice West *(1991), John Maynard describes how "the Sunday crowd celebrated itself—street performers, street crazies, spiritual healers, drug dealers, gang members, bodybuilders, near-naked women, small children, Afghan hounds, chain-saw jugglers, and tourists with expensive cameras, all dodging skaters on neoprene wheels, all accepting each other as completely ordinary, all conspiring to keep the fantasy going."*

A rare quiet moment: early Monday morning the Walk slowly comes back to life after the Sunday revelries.

Of Gamblers, Beats, and Rollerbladers

Venice, which has always attracted a flamboyant crowd, was built shortly after the turn of the century by Abbot Kinney, an eccentric developer who hoped to inspire a cultural renaissance with the Italianate buildings and canals of his version of Venice by the sea.

During its heyday, the town's long spiral pier and the amusements, freak shows, and thrill rides along its midway drew millions. Hotels lined the boardwalk, and bingo and beauty contests took place on the beach.

By the mid-1950s, however, Venice had lost most of its glamour, and its low rents had begun to attract a new clientele. The Beat Generation (with the coffee house as their hub) colonized the beach, followed by flower children, hippies, and other counterculturists. But in 1977, the establishment of the first outdoor-roller-skating shop opened a new chapter for Venice; the carnival atmosphere had returned—on neoprene wheels.

Ocean Drive

Miami Beach, Florida

Ocean Drive is a sweeping seaside promenade located in Miami's South Beach district, but its grand hotels, broad sidewalks, sophisticated open-air cafés, and low stone walls paralleling the white sand beach might be found in one of the beautiful coastal towns of the Mediterranean. Wending the length of the Drive is elegant, palm-dotted Lummus Park. And all around are the luminous, quirky buildings that form Miami's famous Art Deco Architectural District, the youngest historic district in the country.

Undeterred by the Drive's trendiness and the displacement which has ensued, the retirement community continues to use and enjoy nearby Lummus Park.

The sheer number of Art Deco buildings (which extend over an area of twenty blocks) gives Ocean Drive a visual coherence, while the richness of unexpected detail confers lightness and grace. Just a few years ago many of these buildings were slated for demolition, and South Beach was considered one of Miami's most depressed neighborhoods. When developers of the Cardozo Hotel, the area's first major renovation, approached local banks for loans in the late 1970s, they were met with skepticism and turned down. The fight to preserve a handful of small hotels in South Beach excited wide spread interest. Celebrity investors were attracted to the area, and Ocean Drive soon became Miami's most fashionable address.

Although South Beach's trendiness has fueled the preservation of individual buildings, development pressure is increasing. Proposals to build towering, pastel-clad hotels and condominiums, both within and outside the boundaries of the historic district, raise the specter of dislocation for elderly residents

So far, the retirement community has managed to coexist comfortably with the jet-set contingent.

(already displaced once by the gentrification of the Drive's retiree hotels) and the well-established Cuban-American community. These traditional residents of South Beach, who use Lummus Park as a meeting place, keep the area—for the moment, at least—a genuine neighborhood despite the presence of the jet set.

The future of Ocean Drive and the South Beach Art Deco Architectural District depends on the ability of local leaders to balance the needs of tourists with those of residents. In striving to integrate the bikers, rollerbladers, and international glitterati into the mix of retirees and Cuban expatriates, leaders should take a cue from their surroundings: as an architectural form, Art Deco has been democratically applied to the corner gas station and the inexpensive diner as well as to the flamboyant, ocean-side hotels, achieving great diversity within one harmonious style. ■

The stuff that Miami vice is made of: the outdoor cafés along the Drive are expensive and exclusive, but anyone can enjoy the people-watching.

The Struggle for the Heart of Deco

The power of the South Beach Art Deco Architectural District derives from the more than 650 significant buildings dating from the 1930s. As the late Barbara Capitman, the woman responsible for the district's regeneration, has written: "Our Deco is different, plainer, made from cheaper materials...[it] takes its strength from the impact of so many buildings created in the same style."

Capitman, a designer who moved to Miami in the early 1970s, formed the Miami Design Preservation League in 1976 to protect the area from encroaching development. Despite the lack of support from Miami Beach city officials, she succeeded in getting twenty blocks of South Beach territory included on the National Register of Historic Places.

Despite its economic success as an international destination, city leaders are still reluctant to extend stronger protection to South Beach. Like many historic districts that have attracted tourism, South Beach treads a thin line between maintaining its authenticity as a community and building on a brand of success that is also the root of many problems (too many people, boutiques, bars, and restaurants, and, of course, too much traffic). Inclusion on the National Register does not guarantee that a building won't be demolished in the future.

Battery Park City Esplanade

Manhattan, New York

The Esplanade is a remarkably inclusive and tolerant place used by residents of all ages.

Despite the Battery Park City Esplanade's location in the midst of a sleek, impersonal corporate and residential development, it is New York's most successful new public place of the past ten years. Incorporating details reminiscent of Central Park and other beloved New York public places and influenced by the substantial involvement of artists, its uplifting and whimsical design melds art with architecture in the largest and most ambitious application of a one-percent-for-art fund in the country.

The furniture placed along the 70-foot-wide walkway, which follows the Hudson River's edge for more than a mile, is an integral part of the imaginative art works scattered throughout the twenty-five-acre expanse of coves, parks, gardens, playgrounds, and plazas: Walt Whitman's words are inscribed on handrailings, bluestone colonnades frame the river, fountain rims and abstract granite

The success of the Esplanade is in many ways tied to a scruffy path that runs along the Hudson river, from Fourteenth Street to Battery Park. It crosses several residential neighborhoods, and though it never really gets close to the river, it is a popular strolling place that leads people to the Esplanade.

Broken Promises

The remarkable popular success of the Esplanade belies the upper-class residential and corporate enclave of Battery Park City, which is unfriendly and rigidly segregated. Although the original 1968 plan called for low-, middle-, and upper-income apartments, a 1980 revision (ostensibly the result of market constraints) abandoned the commitment to mixed housing.

Instead, a billion dollars was pledged for the construction and rehabilitation of low- and middle-income buildings elsewhere in the city. In all fairness, it must be said that nearly 2,000 units have been renovated in other New York neighborhoods with funds generated by the development. Nonetheless, the possibility of Battery Park City becoming a community that would mirror the diversity of the rest of New York has been eliminated.

sculptures double as seats, and an extravagant rock garden evokes the wilderness of a preindustrial riverbank. The details of the urban landscape— granite hexagonal paving, benches based on designs from the 1939 World's Fair, and lamps copied from old photos—give the Esplanade a human scale and an experiential depth that most of the city's other contemporary parks and plazas lack.

The Esplanade's single greatest draw, though, is the great river itself. Writing in the 1850s, Herman Melville described how New Yorkers liked to walk to the water's edge on Sunday afternoons, "and there they'd stand—miles of them." Lower Manhattan's riverfront has been obstructed for years by highways, ferry buildings, warehouses, and piers. The Esplanade has made it possible once again for thousands of residents from all five boroughs to commune with the river. Their presence makes it what its Battery Park City surroundings are not: a truly diverse place. ■

The Upper Room by Ned Smyth is a colonnaded, open-air court with a gazebo and a long table overlooking the Hudson River.

Courtesy of Ned Smyth.

"City of the world! (for all races are here, all the lands of the earth make contributions here)
City of the Sea! City of wharfs and stores—city of tall facades of marble and iron!
Proud and passionate city—mettlesome, mad, extravagant city!"—Walt Whitman, *City of Ships*, (1865).

A detail of artist Siah Armajani's green enamel and bronze railing, inscribed with Walt Whitman's words about New York. The plaza in front of the World Financial Center is the result of a collaboration between architect Cesar Pelli, landscape architect M. Paul Friedberg, and sculptors Scott Burden and Siah Armajani.

City Within a City

Battery Park City, a 92-acre city within a city by the Hudson River in Lower Manhattan, was built on a site created partly by the excavations for the World Trade Center. The original 1968 concept envisioned a city of the future, completely isolated from the rest of New York, in which a chain of tall buildings clustered around a regional shopping mall were to sit on top of huge parking decks. (One building from the original plan stands as a ghastly reminder of that vision.)

But in the early 1980s, a financial and leadership crisis led the Battery Park City Authority (the entity established to finance, construct, and administer the new community) to drastically revise its concept. The new plan called for developers to work on small parcels of land. They were asked to re-create the spontaneous design of typical downtown streets, reflecting incremental growth at the hands of several architects. And, finally, strict zoning and design guidelines were implemented to give the area a coherent look.

The Esplanade was the first public waterfront park built in New York City since the official opening of the Brooklyn Heights Promenade in 1954.

Main Streets and Places of Commerce

The places in this chapter reflect the rise, fall, and rebirth of Main Street (or Market Street, as it was also called). Once the traditional commercial center of any city, Main Street was a place where homes, offices, banks, hotels, libraries, theaters, and stores containing the best a community had to offer were concentrated in the space of a few blocks. Classic examples of Main Street can be found in Yellow Springs, Ohio, and Madison, Indiana. The former is a typical and unassuming commercial street that has adapted well over time; the latter is a well-preserved avenue of historic buildings that after years of decline has been meticulously restored to its 19th-century beauty.

Country Club Plaza, a pioneering shopping district in Kansas City, Missouri, located miles from the old downtown, is the precursor of today's shopping mall; it is emblematic of Main Street's decline, which was linked to the rise of the automobile. Finally, Boston's Faneuil Hall Marketplace, which resuscitated a dilapidated downtown market district, and Newbury Street, an avenue of art and fashion in the elegant Back Bay section of the city, are proof that commerce can thrive again in old city centers. ■

The 6.5-acre Faneuil Hall Marketplace creates a colorful pedestrian shopping precinct of more than 145 stores and restaurants. The carts that the Marketplace leases to local artists and entrepreneurs were originally intended to be a part of opening-day ceremonies only, but have since become a fixture—and a feature of shopping areas everywhere.

Courtesy of The Rouse Co.

83

Country Club Plaza

Kansas City, Missouri

Today it is hard to appreciate the breadth of vision required of entrepreneur J. C. Nichols back in 1922, when he conceived and developed the country's first shopping mall designed for the automobile, in Kansas City, Missouri. With the construction of Country Club Plaza and the adjacent 5,000-acre residential Country Club District, the self-made developer revolutionized the concept of the American suburb and the way the entire country shopped.

Nichols's genius was in realizing that the automobile was destined to influence not only where urban dwellers shopped and lived but the ways in which suburban communities were built. With Country Club Plaza, he set out to find a new physical form to replace Main Street. By subdividing the area into small blocks with large streets, he sought to improve cars' movements and to maximize the shops' visibility for drivers. Parking in all forms—in the streets, in enclosed courtyards planted with trees, in multistory structures—became an integral part of the plan. Each block was identified by a tower. Gas stations and repair shops were located at key intersections to underscore the obvious preference given to the car.

A 1920s rendering of "Nichols's Folly," the daring development located several miles outside of Kansas City, as it was originally conceived. Visible are the pattern of wide streets and parking squares set in the middle of the blocks, as well as the towers identifying the different parking sections.

Courtesy of The Plaza Merchant's Association.

Although Country Club Plaza is the forerunner of suburban shopping malls throughout the country, it stands apart in both appearance and substance. Its buildings, constructed of the best available materials and designed to last, are decorated with colorful Spanish motifs that provide the complex with a sense of identity and unity. Mature trees, ample sidewalks, awnings, statues, fountains, and sculptures create a harmonious and inviting pedestrian

Despite its name, Country Club Plaza doesn't actually have a plaza. As Nichols reasoned, such a place would only concentrate visitors and cause congestion. The Plaza does, however, have fountains and sculptures located throughout the complex, as well as more than 35 cafés and restaurants.

Hundreds of artists participate in the Plaza Art Fair, which was started as a Depression-era promotion. Held over a three-day weekend in September, the event attracts thousands of visitors.

environment—despite the automobile's dominance.

With the typical life expectancy of current malls limited to twenty years, Country Club Plaza has outlived most of its imitators. Still profitable after 74 years, this once daring shopping center, built in the middle of what was then a cornfield, has become a venerable landmark and a tribute to a successful effort to merge ideals of contemporary civic culture with the needs of an increasingly car-dependent society. ∎

Nichols's Folly

In 1922, when J. C. Nichols announced his intention to build a shopping complex of 250 stores on 55 acres adjacent to his residential Country Club District development, Kansas City's leaders branded it "Nichols's Folly." The site—in the countryside three miles south of the city's center—was thought to be too remote for so large a project. But Nichols realized that customers would be drawn to a shopping center tied to Kansas City's growing network of motorways and boulevards; as parking in town became increasingly limited, he predicted, drivers would go elsewhere rather than take the streetcar. By the time Nichols died, in 1950, the Country Club Plaza and District had become celebrated archetypes for the automobile suburb.

Faneuil Hall Marketplace

Boston, Massachusetts

Courtesy of The Rouse Co.

The old cobblestone walkways in front of Boston's historic Quincy Market have been landscaped with trees, benches, colored lights, and banners.

It is easy to dismiss Faneuil Hall as just another of the many festival marketplaces that have sprung up, with mixed fortunes, across the country: certainly it has lost its edge, and in the twenty years since it originated the trend, it has come to resemble a suburban mall relocated in the center of Boston. But to dismiss Faneuil Hall would be overlook its many groundbreaking contributions and the tremendous impact it has had on the livability of many other cities.

The Marketplace broke all industry rules when it was built, in 1976: it had no air-conditioning, no free parking, and no major department store to anchor it. In fact, the developers deliberately steered clear of big-name retail stores in favor of small, local businesses—an approach so unorthodox that Boston's Mayor Kevin White, a major supporter of the project, had to twist more than one banker's arm to ensure the project's financing, as well as arrange for the city to put up a third of the cost.

The idea of turning the old Quincy Market (three abandoned early-nineteenth-century sheds that were nearly demolished in 1961) into a retail center was daunting: to work, it had to generate $150 in sales per square foot—twice the volume of Boston's biggest department stores and equal to the most profitable suburban malls. The marketing concept was to create an atmosphere of gusto and excitement by bringing together many small, interesting shops offering an extraordinary variety of merchandise and high-quality food vendors selling fresh, ready-to-eat gourmet food—all within the confines of a contained historic downtown area. And it worked: the Marketplace succeeded in outdoing all estimates, with a sales volume of $233 per square foot in the first year, and a staggering $500 per square foot in the years that followed.

Something much larger than the success of a specific marketing concept was at stake here, however: the decrepit downtowns of older cities had long been given up on, and Faneuil Hall tested the very idea that they could be revived. But with its unmatched sales figures and genuine opening-day excitement, the Marketplace became the first nationally recognized success at doing so and gave new hope to communities of all sizes. On that first day, the small crowd that gathered for the morning ceremonies grew throughout the day to some 100,000 people. In its first year, some ten million people visited the Marketplace—as many as visited Disneyland. The "Faneuilization of America" had begun. ∎

An American Original

The Faneuil Hall Marketplace was a project whose time had come. Its reuse of the historic Quincy Market buildings was in keeping with the country's emerging rediscovery of its architectural past. The preservation movement, started as a last-ditch effort to save historic buildings from the bulldozer, had begun to turn its attention toward the rescue of entire historic areas. Latimer Square, in Denver; the Strand, in Galveston; and Pioneer Square, in Seattle, for example—preservation projects that generated great popular interest—were all being developed at the same time as Faneuil Hall.

In addition, a food revolution in the early 1970s was widening the nation's culinary horizons, and the Market's food vendors were able to cater to a newly acquired taste for gourmet food. Americans were discovering new, adventurous foods from Europe and Asia and acquiring an appreciation for the fresh, local products available only at public markets. Faneuil Hall's sidewalk restaurants evoked the pleasures of Parisian café life for a generation of travelers abroad.

The genius of Faneuil Hall Marketplace was in bringing these elements together, in a single location, in 1976. In doing so it awakened the hedonist slumbering deep inside America and, in the process, reaped extraordinary profits.

Courtesy of The Rouse Co.

An aerial view of Faneuil Hall shows the market's central structure, which is reserved for food vendors, flanked by arcades devoted to small specialty boutiques.

Newbury Street

Boston, Massachusetts

Newbury Street, located in Boston's exclusive Back Bay district, represents a new breed of shopping district that capitalizes on its historic character while carving a distinctive marketing niche—in this case one focusing on arts and fashion. Newbury's complex mix of boutiques, galleries, and exclusive hotels, complemented by a tight web of supporting businesses (fashion photographers' studios, modeling agencies, print and beauty shops), makes it a place where fashion is not only sold but made. Commercial rents are among the highest in the country, and its shops attract affluent tourists from around the world.

One of the remarkable aspects of Newbury Street is how well its pedestrian and residential scale has survived, despite having lost its former atmosphere of neighborly tranquillity to the bustle of traffic and

Art, created in studios and on the sidewalks, is a part of everyday life on Newbury Street.

commerce. When the street was developed, in 1853, strict and forward-looking land-use and zoning prescriptions were established in great detail regarding the height, building materials, and layout of the structures, and those guidelines were retained in the 1920s, when new commercial buildings replaced

The beautiful brick buildings of Newbury Street give it a competitive edge over upscale suburban shopping malls, which can neither replicate its elegance and history, nor create the residential and commercial diversity found there.

An Eclectic Place

The architectural character of Newbury Street was determined by the strict building and land-use regulations established for the Back Bay, a landfill development created in 1853 to be a solely residential, private enclave for Boston's elite. Since the development excluded industry from the entire area and commercial establishments from the development's main boulevard, Commonwealth Avenue, the many cultural institutions that followed the upper-class Bostonians to the new neighborhood settled on Newbury Street, setting it apart from the rest of the district. The Massachusetts Institute of Technology's first home and the museum for the Boston Society of Natural History were both located on Newbury, as were several churches and a temple. By 1890, there were four schools and four hotels along the street's eight-block stretch. These developments changed the private, residential nature of Newbury and injected it with the eclectic diversity that characterizes it today.

some of the older residential ones. Dominated by tall church spires and rows of elegant 19th-century four-story homes that have been converted into offices, studios, and shops, it looks essentially the same as it does in turn-of-the-century photographs. ∎

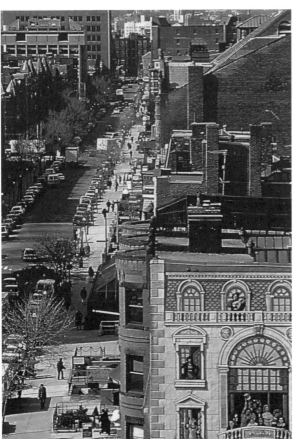

An aerial view of the street clearly announces the dominant role the arts play on Newbury Street. In the foreground is a mural entitled "Let Every Man Practice the Art He Knows," an architectural extravaganza depicting famous people and famous works of art.

Xenia Avenue
and Main Street

Xenia Avenue, Yellow Springs, Ohio
Main Street, Madison, Indiana

An historic building, a tall tree, a bookstore, a setback, and a bench create a special corner on Xenia Avenue.

Xenia Avenue is an unpretentious boulevard in Yellow Springs, Ohio, where it's typical to see a John Deere tractor parked next to a mountain bike. Main Street, in Madison, Indiana, is a showcase of 19th-century Midwestern commercial and residential architecture. The two couldn't be more different in character, yet they both express the variety and resilience of the small town main street while also demonstrating its vulnerability.

Xenia Avenue extends for just a few blocks, but it provides all of the basic necessities for this rural college town of 4,000. Most residents make several informal trips daily to the downtown area, which begins at the first stoplight on Xenia and ends at the last, with a few historic gems sprinkled among the modest commercial buildings. The pace is slow on weekdays, but recently tourists— drawn by such nearby attractions as Glen Helen, a nature preserve, and by the quaint atmosphere of Yellow Springs itself—have begun to invade the town on weekends, a disruption compounded by the fact that Xenia is a leg of U.S. Route 66, a north-south shortcut between Columbus and Cincinnati.

Tourism has also had consequences for Main Street in Madison, Indiana. As the core of a downtown historic district on the shores of the Ohio River, it was one of first sites selected for the prestigious Main Street Program, sponsored by the National Trust for Historic Preservation in the 1970s. With the assistance of local financing, the program adopted an incremental strategy to renovate the

Under the watchful eyes of adults, Xenia Avenue's sidewalks double as a playground for young residents.

buildings along Main Street, then in a state of severe disrepair. Cleaning the brick walls and exposing fluted cast-iron columns with flared capitals (long covered with plastic and aluminum signs) not only revealed Madison's distinctive architectural style but also created a positive climate for reinvestment in the old Main Street.

The renovation brought citizens back downtown and renewed a sense of pride and ownership that had almost totally dissipated. But along with a certain predictability in the type of merchandise the Main Street stores offer (souvenirs, antiques),

In addition to the local hardware store, Xenia Avenue is home to: one drugstore, several banks, an independent supermarket, a natural-foods store, a bicycle-rental shop, a variety store, the offices of the local newspaper, two bookstores, the senior center, one coffee shop, and one trendy restaurant.

The Madison Look

Madison's distinctive architecture emerged in the city during a sustained construction boom that took place between 1820 and 1860 and blended Federal, Classical, Gothic Revival, and Italianate styles. By the time they'd arrived in Madison from the East and the South, none of these styles was necessarily pure, and as the side-by-side structures were built they borrowed from each other, as well.

In the 1860s, cast iron became the standard remodeling material for the storefronts along Main Street, and such elements as columns and sheet-metal cornices, produced by local industries, added an indigenous touch to the already eclectic Madison look. Today, all 133 blocks of the downtown district are included in the National Register of Historic Places.

Flower beds and benches make Main Street in Madison, Indiana, a restful and pleasant place to visit.

tourism has also brought the possibility of displacement for establishments serving the resident population.

Now is a defining moment for Xenia Avenue and Main Street, as they try to maintain their authenticity and their status as the commercial and social focus of their respective towns while also struggling with such problems as traffic, tourists, or the opening of the next superstore nearby. ■

The rhythmic detailing of the brick and cast-iron facades give Main Street in Madison a sense of unity, despite the wide variety of architectural styles.

Opposite: A view of Madison from the shores of the Ohio River, a source of steamboat trade in the 1820s that made Madison a midwestern port of entry for homesteaders and one of Indiana's most prosperous communities.

Photo by Sally McWilliams. Courtesy of Main Street Project.

Outdoor Living Rooms

The living room is a shared space where the members of a household congregate, play, take care of business. On a grander scale, the five places in this chapter serve the same purpose for city residents, providing a common ground—an outdoor living room—where the community can meet in celebration or confrontation, in matters of business, or simply for the sake of social recreation. All five are flexible in their uses and exceedingly well maintained and designed.

The Promenade and Plaza at Rockefeller Center, in Manhattan, are the closest thing that New York City has to a town square. On the Columbia University campus, the Low Memorial Library Steps provide the student body with a social arena for both serious and frivolous pursuits. Bryant Park, in Manhattan, and Post Office Square, in Boston, are glorious new gathering places for city workers (the former the recipient of a transformative renovation, the latter built from scratch). They offer valuable lessons on how to involve the private sector in restoring high-quality public places or creating new ones. Finally, Washington Square, in San Francisco, is a superb example of a neighborhood park that is peacefully shared by a diverse group of residents. ∎

Bryant Park is kept scrupulously clean, thanks to a combination of selective, well-thought-out rules, unobtrusive policing, and regular maintenance of the furniture, flower beds, and lawns.

Bryant Park

Manhattan, New York

On either side of the Great Lawn are 300-foot-long, 12-foot-deep perennial borders—one of the more intricately designed and better maintained flower displays in the city.

Redefined by its new design, Bryant Park no longer attempts to transport the visitor to some imaginary Arcadian landscape: the city is visible everywhere. The $8.9 million, five-year renovation project was financed primarily by the Rockefeller Brothers Fund, and by companies that had offices overlooking the Park.

Bryant Park, backyard to the New York Public Library, is one of the most sensual, graceful open spaces in New York City. Facing the Edwardian rear facade of the library, it draws office workers, shoppers, and out-of-town visitors—more than 10,000 people each day—to its sunny lawn, adorned with spectacular flowering perennial borders and flanked by allées lined with tall plane trees. Until recently, though, it was known as "needle park" for the drug dealers who once patronized it.

The key to Bryant Park's resurgence has been its redesign—possibly the finest application of the observation and rehabilitation techniques pioneered by William H. Whyte, author of the seminal work *City; Rediscovering the Center*, and the main catalyst in the Park's renaissance. His approach to the renovation of the six-acre site hinged on making the interior more visible and accessible. The walls were lowered, new entrances were added and the original ones were widened, and the tall shrubs that had inadvertently served as a screen for drug deals were eliminated. Openings were made in the raised stone balustrade so that the park could be crossed from all directions. Replicas of the original 1930s lamps were installed, and floodlights were introduced for extra security at night. But the greatest touch—suggested by Whyte—was the addition of 2,000 green wood-and-metal folding chairs, which complement the more traditional stationary benches. The chairs transform the several food kiosks into spacious outdoor cafés, and, doubled up, serve as tables for alfresco lunches. They turn the lawn, a more contained and elegant version of Central Park's Great Lawn, into a theater of shifting stage sets.

The Park's management is in the hands of the Bryant Park Restoration Corporation, a privately funded group formed to lead the renovation effort and one of a new breed of nonprofit organizations that are being set up in cities everywhere to care for public parks. Using money from an assessment on nearby properties and revenues from on-site concessions, the Corporation spends close to $2 million annually to keep the Park clean and the flowers blooming. And by providing this beautiful city park with an economic engine to sustain its landscape—a necessity that past redesign plans overlooked—it has also brought what appears to be the permanent return of a thankful public. ∎

The civilized behavior of patrons reflects the high degree of care given to the Park.

It's All in the Details

The first major redesign of Bryant Park, undertaken by Robert Moses in 1934, turned what was left of the decayed original 1871 Victorian version into a formal, if not cold, Beaux Arts public garden. The seed of the park's future failure, however, was sewn into its design. The ideal that Moses pursued was a setting of "restful beauty," physically removed from the bustle of the surrounding midtown streets. Unfortunately, as William H. Whyte has pointed out, with few entrances, no diagonal walkways, and a vast unused lawn enclosed by restraining balustrades, the park discouraged the casual pedestrian from entering. Raising the park above street level and enclosing it with an iron fence, dense shrubbery, and trees made the grounds even more inhospitable. In time, the concealed quiet of the park proved most desirable to winos, vagrants, and drug dealers.

Numerous strategies to rid the park of these people were considered. A typical plan called for more police; another was to drastically limit the park's hours. It was even suggested that the park be entered only from the library, by those with library cards, which was, of course, unacceptably exclusionary. All of these tactics fell short, however, because they failed to consider the alienating effect of the park's design and did not offer a way to entice the public back.

Post Office Square

Boston, Massachusetts

A view of the central lawn from under the wooden trellises.

"Although it was built in the late 20th century, Post Office Square's allusions to 19th-century forms seem to evoke a genteel behavior not typical in parks today."

Joan Goody from her letter of nomination

In the heart of Boston's financial district, on a site previously occupied by an old, dysfunctional concrete parking structure, stands Post Office Square—a lush new 1.7-acre park built on top of a nearly invisible 1,400-space underground parking garage. The creation of such a beautiful and thoughtfully designed new public place in the crowded, costly center of Boston is surprising in this era of civic disinvestment, yet Post Office Square has quickly become an exalted landmark and a reference point in the district's otherwise confusing street grid.

The park owes its existence to the economic savvy of a group called Friends of Post Office Square, local property owners who formulated and implemented the financial strategy, and to the political muscle of City Hall officials, who exercised eminent domain to condemn the decrepit above-ground garage. Both sides benefited: the business community got rid of

Every inch of grass is occupied at lunch hour.

A Square Deal

Post Office Square shows what can happen when business interests, political foresight (that is, the willingness of politicians to trade immediate gain for long-term benefits), and intelligent planning join forces. Many decisions brought about the construction of the new park and underground garage at Post Office Square, but the most important was made by Mayor Raymond L. Flynn, who rejected a 1982 proposal to build a high-rise office building, which guaranteed short-term revenues, in favor of the far riskier (and far more costly) plan to develop a public square with underground parking.

The project was paid for entirely with private funds. Friends of Post Office Square, a group of local property owners and tenants, issued an initial stock offering of 450 shares at $65,000 each. The stock raised $29 million and sold rapidly, mostly to the owners themselves, who then secured a $60 million loan.

With financing in place, Friends of Post Office Square bought the lease of the old garage (which its owner refused to sell until 1987) and purchased the land from the city for $1 million. Though the new garage opened in 1990, at a time when Boston's downtown real-estate market was in a recession, a combination of aggressive marketing, premium location, and quality design brought the garage to full occupancy within a few months of its inauguration. The park opened two years later, in 1992.

an eyesore and saw local property values rise dramatically, while the City of Boston acquired a new park. Once all debts are retired, the lucrative garage will belong to the city, which meanwhile receives all yearly profits from the venture.

The ultimate winners, though, are the citizens of Boston, who can now spend their lunch hour away from the pressures of work, in a glorious park furnished with cast-iron benches, trellised walkways, and more than 125 varieties of trees and shrubs. Post Office Square is, essentially, a triangular urban room, enclosed by the ornate facades of several of Boston's most notable buildings (including the Post Office, the Meridien Hotel, and the New England Telephone Building). In this protected environment, where the sound of two fountains muffles the noise of the surrounding streets, it is easy to forget that just below operates the Square's economic engine— seven floors of underground parking. ■

The focal point of the park is a glass-and-bronze fountain sculpture designed by Rhode Island artist Howard Ben Tré. It is especially popular with young children.

Washington Square

San Francisco, California

An aerial view of Washington Square, taken from the top of Coit Tower, shows, in the words of one panelist, "how urban parks should be—simple, open, integrated into the neighborhoods they serve, and with a well defined perimeter. This is a lesson we often forget."

Washington Square is a quintessential neighborhood park, located at the conjunction of three distinct neighborhoods—Little Italy, Chinatown, and Telegraph Hill—in San Francisco's North Beach district. Its present layout, which dates from 1955 (the square itself was established in 1847), is memorable for the simplicity of its design: a large central lawn, unbroken by formal paths, is open to the sky and encircled by a shady bench-lined pathway. The park lies in a valley between Telegraph Hill and Russian Hill and offers panoramic views of the 19th- and 20th-century frame buildings that seem to march down the slopes toward the park.

This visual connection with the surrounding neighborhoods serves to strengthen residents' sense of ownership of the park, which is also the cultural hub of the neighborhood. The Church of St. Peter and St. Paul, the Italian Men's Athletic Club,

On a typical morning residents share Washington Square, enjoying a quiet moment on the benches that ring the park.

and the Pagoda Theater (which screens Chinese-language movies) are just a few of the landmarks that exemplify the pluralistic nature of the park's constituency. Weddings, funeral services, tai-chi classes for seniors, school outings, and children's play dates take place in the Square, which is also enjoyed by the patrons of the bohemian cafés that face the park (and for which North Beach is famous). ■

Tai-chi exercises are performed on the lawn.

A Neighborhood Park

In a city known for its many great parks and recreation areas, there are remarkably few neighborhood places. An exception is Washington Square, which occupies one city block. In fact, of the three urban parks shown in San Francisco's 1847 city plan, only Washington Square remains intact. The creation of the North Beach Playground one block north, in 1910, spared the park from being turned into playing fields. Though it sits at the crossroads of several popular tourist destinations (Chinatown, Coit Tower, Little Italy, Fisherman's Wharf), fortunate circumstances have preserved the residential nature of the surrounding district and kept the park central to the neighborhood.

The Promenade and Plaza

Rockefeller Center, Manhattan, New York

A s symbols of New York City, the Rockefeller Center Promenade and Plaza are equal in stature to the Empire State Building and the Statue of Liberty. The Promenade, a gently sloping pedestrian street off New York's Fifth Avenue, is lined with elegant shops, reflecting pools, and a series of exquisitely landscaped raised garden beds. It leads to the Plaza, a sunken courtyard surrounded by a ring of tall, brilliantly colored flags, which is used for dining in summer and for skating in the winter. This crowded, fun, pedestrian environment is visited by more than 175,000 people every day.

Together the Promenade and Plaza form the core of the original Rockefeller Center, the grand, Depression-era 14-building development in midtown Manhattan—possibly the finest urban complex ever built in the United States. The fact that it is private property is countered by its design, which has made the transition from the public avenue to the private space almost imperceptible by bringing the Manhattan street grid right into the Center and echoing the character of Fifth Avenue in style and building materials. In being connected to the city's subway system, the Center is also linked to residents of the entire region.

The care lavished on the Promenade and Plaza has made them more accessible than most of the city's public areas, many of which are not maintained properly. In this pristine, almost magical corner of the city, snow disappears before it turns to gray slush and the flowers are replaced before they whither. The garden displays—which change as often as fourteen

The Promenade has provided generations of visitors with a quintessential New York experience. It has always been a lively, safe place, even during the 1960s and early 1970s, when public places everywhere were neglected and vandalized.

Courtesy of Rockefeller Center.

Courtesy of Rockefeller Center.

Both tourists and residents love to ice-skate at Rockefeller Center's rink, cheered on by spectators from all over the world.

times a year—mark the passage of seasons, highlight major events and holidays, and make a visit to Rockefeller Center a pleasant surprise, even for longtime residents.

As an example of what enlightened self-interest and audacious capitalism can achieve, Rockefeller Center—a relatively tiny spot—has made a big impact on urban design. Few places in the country have been conceived with such vision and ambition. Even fewer are so intelligently maintained. ■

Photo by Bart Barlow. Courtesy of Rockefeller Plaza.

Skating at the Plaza

Rockefeller Center had its origins in plans for an uptown home for the Metropolitan Opera, which in 1928 was located in inadequate facilities at Broadway and 39th Street. Early drawings depicted a grand plaza surrounded by towers facing the new opera house, with a shopping promenade spread over three blocks west of Fifth Avenue. The stock-market crash of 1929 squelched the Metropolitan's plans, however, and left John D. Rockefeller, Jr. with several blocks of run-down real estate on his hands. He quickly revamped the original plan's cultural center, turning it into a major business and shopping complex.

When shoppers proved reluctant to patronize the sunken shopping plaza, a new use had to be found. The outdoor skating rink—which has, possibly, contributed the most to Rockefeller Center's success—was introduced, as a temporary measure, on Christmas Day in 1936. Since then, skating at the Plaza, in the slightly surreal setting of glimmering business towers, has become a Christmas tradition shared by generations of New Yorkers and visitors.

A symbol of New York's cosmopolitan aspirations, the Promenade provides an elegant retreat from Fifth Avenue at the point where it becomes most crowded. Behind it are the Plaza and the entrance to the RCA Building, Rockefeller Center's tallest structure, which has great style without being intrusive—a quality absent from the Center's post-World War II expansion, west of Sixth Avenue.

Low Memorial Library Steps

Columbia University, Manhattan, New York

Photo by Daniel T. Seginak.

Mixing the pursuits of sun worship (top) and commerce (bottom right), students at Columbia University demonstrate the Steps' ability to accommodate a wide variety of activities.

"The Steps are as close in feeling to the Spanish Steps in Rome as anything in this country, certainly in New York."

From the panel discussion.

Although the Low Memorial Library Steps at Columbia University are set against the formal backdrop of the 1897 Low Memorial Library—one of New York's most beautiful colonnaded Beaux Arts buildings—the atmosphere is informal and animated. Not only do the Steps get one from the street level to the Library entrance, they also serve as a device to connect the south side of the campus to the terraced north side, a kind of felicitous social bottleneck where the meeting of friends is an inevitable occurrence.

Located just off the University's main entrance, the Steps are used in an infinite number of ways. Some (reading, working, conversing) seem consistent with the University's image as the "city of learning," while others (sleeping, sunbathing, and kissing) show why the steps have become known among students as the "urban beach."

The original intent of Columbia's architect, Charles Follon McKim, was to integrate the University (now enclosed and gated) with the rest of the city. He

Architect Robert A. M. Stern has made a succinct case for the value of the Low Library Steps: "The Steps have a remarkable capacity to inspire. If we stop making that kind of space, we're in trouble."

City of Learning

When Columbia decided in 1892 to move its tiny campus from East 49th Street to a six-block expanse between 114th and 120th Streets on Broadway, it commissioned master plans from three different architects. Charles Coolidge Haight and Richard Morris Hunt each presented designs in which the buildings, clustered around small courtyards, effectively insulated the University from its neighborhood. Charles Follon McKim, however, took a wider view of the University's role. His aggressively urban Beaux Arts plan acknowledged the cosmopolitan character of the site and proposed that buildings be constructed along city streets and avenues, and that the campus be open to the Manhattan street grid. That decision, along with the idea of integrating the campus into the city, shaped the urban American university for years to come.

envisioned the Steps as the heart of the campus and the campus as the heart of the neighborhood.

If McKim were to visit Columbia today, he might be surprised by some of the ways in which the Steps are used, but he would certainly recognize their role as the cour d'honneur (ceremonial court) of the campus. ■

Public Squares

When European settlers began building towns in the New World, they modeled them on the Old World cities they had left behind, in which the public plaza played a pivotal role in civic life. The places in this chapter trace the public square's evolution into an indigenous American type.

The plazas of the Spanish colonial settlements are most closely related to the European model. Although much altered today, El Pueblo in Los Angeles is undergoing a renaissance, as a result of an influx of Mexican-Americans in the region. La Plaza de Santa Fe, in New Mexico, is, possibly, the best-preserved Spanish square in the country. Although it has been the center of life in Santa Fe for hundreds of years, it is slowly losing that role as tourists take over. In Connecticut, the New Haven Green is an example of the type of public place that the English settlers placed at the heart of their communities: the grazing and parade ground, or common, around which the town's church, city hall, and civic institutions were built. Finally, in Sidney, Ohio, and Oxford, Mississippi, we find two outstanding examples of the distinctively American public square that evolved as Americans moved westward and southward in the 19th century. ∎

Several monuments document Santa Fe Plaza's turbulent history; today its comfortable wrought-iron benches and well-watered lawns are a magnet for weary tourists.

The Green

New Haven, Connecticut

The formal paths traversing the Green are etched into the snow after a winter storm. Along a central divide stand three churches built between 1812 and 1814.

The New Haven Green is an exquisite urban place that has survived the tide of progress with its 19th-century form miraculously intact. Its rigorous, formal beauty reflects the puritan moral code of the New England settlers who created it. Yet, despite the lure of its luxuriant lawns and mature trees, and its central location next to Yale University and Chapel Street (New Haven's busiest avenue), the Green has never been a popular place.

Part of the Green's current lack of appeal can be ascribed to its size: at seventeen acres, it is too big to be intimate, too small and formal to be a city park. In addition, in the 1970s an ill-conceived urban renewal plan drastically changed the scale and character of its perimeter. The southern side was cleared to make way for an enclosed shopping mall that, while not particularly successful (it is perennially on the brink of economic collapse), saps the area's commercial energy and draws people off the streets. The eastern side of the Green was reorganized into a superblock of tall office buildings and blank sidewalks that are not conducive to street life. Finally, on top of all the urban renewal, Yale's Old Campus, on the west side, siphons students away from the Green with its own private and, presumably, safer squares.

Occasionally, the Green comes into its own: during occasional summertime concerts and Yale's commencement exercises its formal and ceremonial beauty are used to great advantage. The rest of the time, however, the Green is admired at a distance as a textbook example of traditional American urbanism, a celebrated public place waiting to be discovered. ■

A formal fence encloses the north side of the Green, where New Haven's public library and courthouse generate the park's only civic and pedestrian interest.

Common Law

The New Haven Green is legally a private property, a rare if not unique relic of Colonial times, when the central space of a community was held collectively by the town's property owners. Laid out in 1638 according to the Roman nine-square grid, New Haven's common belonged to those with shares in the town's original venture.

In the 1680s, the Connecticut Assembly passed these rights down to the shareholders' descendants, who were now no longer synonymous with the town's government. In 1724, the descendants met for the first time as the Proprietors of Common and Undivided Lands, but by 1805 they had become so dispersed that the remaining Proprietors turned over their powers and privileges, in perpetuity, to a committee of five of their members—though at the time the practice in New England was to bequeath ownership of the common to local governing bodies. Nevertheless, with the state legislature's approval, the five Proprietors became a self-perpetuating institution, replacing their members as they saw fit. They own the New Haven Green to this day.

The Plaza

Santa Fe, New Mexico

The unique and ancient Plaza de Santa Fe has been the center of this city's public life for almost 400 years. The warmth of its mud, timber, and stone architecture is so welcoming to visitors, however, that in the short span of twenty years the Plaza has been completely overtaken by tourists. The square is crowded and full of activity all day long, but Santa Fe residents, put off by a homogenous and distracted crowd of tourist gawkers and shoppers, seldom venture there.

The Native American open-air market, spread out in the shade of the Governor's Palace, is a popular draw for tourists. The quality of the jewelry may be questionable, but the tradition itself is as old as the Santa Fe Trail, which opened up trade in the West.

This phenomenon, which has driven out indispensable local shops around the square (with the exception of Woolworths) and replaced them with a predictable mix of national-chain retailers and upscale boutiques, extends well beyond the square itself: the historic core of Santa Fe has become a massive shopping mall disguised in adobe garb.

Residents, now deprived of practical reasons to be on the Plaza, avoid it, even though many of the city's main civic and cultural institutions (the post office, the library, and several museums) are only a block away.

There are no simple solutions to the daily invasion. Tourism is a major part of the local economy, and the Plaza, with its tremendous historic and aesthetic magnetism, will always be a major attraction. To reclaim their square (and by extension their city), residents and leaders of Santa Fe must redefine their priorities in order to balance the demands of tourism with the protection of their own quality of life. In the past, they have shown great

The Plaza is at its best in the crisp morning hours, after cleaning crews have erased the results of the previous day's abuse. Visitors wander in with newspapers and cups of exotic coffee and find seats on the wrought-iron benches. For a few hours, the Plaza functions as the center of this beautiful and unique city.

strength and clarity of purpose in this area—the city's strict design guidelines, for example, have preserved the authenticity of the local architectural style. Applied to the management of tourism, such commitment and single-mindedness will restore the Plaza to its place at the center of the community's civic life. ∎

An aerial view of the city depicts the Plaza and the important civic buildings that surround it. The ancient cottonwoods, fed by the Acequia Madre (the "mother ditch") flowing through the center of town, provide refuge from the intense sun.

With Sun, Straw, and Mud

Rather than any individual building, it is the extensive use of adobe that makes Santa Fe such a memorable visual experience. Introduced by Franciscan missionaries in the 17th century, the sun-dried mud-and-straw bricks, with their tawny palette, resonate with the surrounding desert.

The now famous Santa Fe style, which has been assiduously protected by area residents, comes from an architectural heritage that melded the distinct cultural building styles of the Pueblo Indians, the Franciscan missionaries, and the Spanish colonialists. Early in the 20th century, writers, archaeologists, and artists, hearing rumors of the Southwest's extraordinary natural beauty and its precolonial and colonial cultures, began to settle in Santa Fe. Sensitive to the area's riches, they sought to preserve and restore the indigenous architecture and to revive in their own homes various local styles. Their efforts culminated in a 1957 law which limited building in the historic district (which includes most of the heavily built areas of the city) to the Spanish Pueblo Revival and Territorial Revival styles. The result is an architecture that is at times reminiscent of the multistoried setbacks of the pueblos, at others of the timbered Spanish Colonial buildings (represented most notably by the Governor's Palace, erected in 1610).

El Pueblo de Los Angeles

Los Angeles, California

On Sunday afternoons, the site of Los Angeles's first settlement, El Pueblo de Los Angeles, undergoes a dazzling metamorphosis from a worn-down, slightly dispirited tourist attraction into the hub of a vibrant community. Mexican-Americans from all over the region come to El Pueblo to attend mass at the Plaza Catholic Church, the city's oldest house of worship. Afterwards, people gather spontaneously in the narrow streets and plazas, visiting with friends and meeting relatives. The unparalleled spirit of this weekly ritual is bringing new life to this little-known historic district.

In a sea of towering downtown corporate offices, El Pueblo is an island of small-scale, pedestrian-oriented buildings. Its intimacy, which suggests the city before the arrival of the automobile and skyscraper, is ideal for the public life that erupts there with abandon each Sunday. The central Old Plaza (dating to 1781) and the traditional stall-lined market street of Olvera (which is nearly as old) teem with

Don Francisco Avila's 1818 adobe (pictured here) is one of the town houses built around El Pueblo's plazas by wealthy Mexican ranchers of the time. Twenty-seven buildings from this period still stand in the area surrounding the Old Plaza.

people, food vendors weave through the crowds, outdoor restaurants are full, and small groups cluster around benches.

El Pueblo fills an important gap in the life of the Mexican-American community. By providing a place where they can freely speak their native tongue and celebrate the traditional events of their civic and religious calendar, it unifies a scattered community and links them with their history as settlers of early Los Angeles.

If the Mexican-American population continues to grow, as has been predicted, El Pueblo's role will

El Pueblo reflects the ongoing family history of many in the Mexican-American community of Los Angeles.

undoubtedly expand. Although the district is in need of a major face-lift, its future looks bright. It has been included in a redevelopment plan—along with historic Union Station, Chinatown, Little Tokyo, and East Los Angeles—that is likely to provide the humble founding place of this vast metropolis with new business and cultural opportunities, not just on Sunday but on every day of the week. ■

The major Mexican festivals of Cinco de Mayo, Día de Los Muertos, and the Christmas Las Posadas take place on the Old Plaza, which is a natural gathering spot on Sundays. El Pueblo de la Reina de Los Angeles was founded here in 1781, by order of the King of Spain.

A Sterling Effort

It is largely through one woman's efforts that so much of Los Angeles's original town has survived. Christine Sterling, who lived on the Old Plaza, began El Pueblo's preservation in 1926, with a crusade to save the Avila Adobe, the city's oldest dwelling. With the help of influential friends, she rallied local newspapers to her cause and raised enough money not only to restore and turn the Avila house into a museum, but to rebrick Olvera, colonial Los Angeles's market street.

Sterling worked to restore the 19th-century buildings of the Old Plaza, where many of Los Angeles's richest inhabitants, subjects of Spain and then of Mexico, once had their homes. In 1930, Olvera Street was transformed into a Mexican marketplace, where craftspeople and restaurateurs were installed in many of the buildings.

Courthouse Squares

Sidney, Ohio
Oxford, Mississippi

Several of the commercial buildings overlooking Oxford's Courthouse Square, such as the Square Books café, have easily accessible second-floor porches, which add a pleasurable dimension to doing business on the Square.

An aerial view of Oxford's Courthouse square, the geographical and political center of town since 1837.

In Sidney, Ohio, and in Oxford, Mississippi, the courthouse square is the undisputed center of the community; in both cities, it showcases the best public architecture and embodies the town character, while thriving as a downtown, a government center, a main street, and a meeting place.

Oxford's down-to-earth square was conceived by its founders as a sober and utilitarian place of business. Indeed, its character was preordained: when the boundary lines of Lafayette County were laid down, in 1837, with Oxford as its seat, they were determined "according to the distance a man could travel by horseback or wagon from his farm to the courthouse—leaving at daylight, attending to his business, and returning home by dark." In more recent times, the presence of the University of Mississippi, whose 7,000 students live within walking distance of the square, has encouraged the

Three men enjoy a quiet moment in front of the courthouse that William Faulkner helped preserve.

"They Call This Progress..."

Oxford, Mississippi, was William Faulkner's hometown, and it appeared often in his prose. He modeled the seat of his fictional county, Yoknapatawpha, on Oxford. And in Requiem for a Nun, *he described the courthouse as "the center, the focus, the hub; sitting looming in the center of the county's circumference like a single cloud in its ring of horizon... protector of the weak, judiciate and curb of the passions and lusts, repository and guardian of the aspirations and the hopes."*

Over the years, Faulkner kept an eye on Courthouse Square. In a 1947 letter to the Oxford Eagle *protesting the threatened demolition of the Lafayette Courthouse, Faulkner lamented the destruction of the buildings and places that defined his town: "We have gotten rid of the shade trees that once circled the courthouse yard and bordered the Square itself...all we have left now to distinguish an old Southern town from any one of ten-thousand towns from Kansas to California are the Confederate Monument, the courthouse, and the jail...They call this progress but they don't say where it is going."*

growth of a small shopping district that includes a handful of shops, galleries, restaurants, and a good bookstore. (Square Books is a gathering place for residents and visiting intellectuals.) By supplying pleasures the founders seem to have overlooked, these merchants have extended the life of the square beyond regular business hours and well into the evening.

The most striking aspect of Sidney's Courthouse Square is its architecture. From the ornate French Second Empire courthouse to the eclectic private

On the southwest corner stands Louis Sullivan's Peoples Federal Savings and Loan Association. "A major work of architecture, by a highly individualistic and expressive architect, [it] is absolutely in keeping with the scale and topology of its urban setting." Alan J. Plattus, from his letter of nomination.

115

commercial buildings along the perimeter, the consistently high quality of the architecture is a testament to the civic leaders, merchants, and bankers who viewed the buildings they erected not only as functional commodities or as a means for promoting their businesses but as embellishment to the town that would have strong impact on its streets and squares. One of Louis Sullivan's most famous rural banks, the Peoples Federal Savings and Loan Association, is located here. Considered a masterpiece, it is a thoroughly original building that nevertheless blends well with its neighbors.

Both squares are flourishing commercial districts. Because they offer more than just shopping, they have weathered economic decline better than most downtowns. They provide a complex web of complementary businesses and retail shops of various sizes. In Oxford, for example, the local department store stands side by side with small apparel and antique shops.

In a simple, unaffected way, Sidney and Oxford have preserved two examples of one of America's most enduring public icons—the courthouse square—capitalizing on their beauty and economic diversity without turning them into tourist attractions or museum pieces. ∎

A stroll around Sidney's Courthouse Square takes one past buildings that reflect 150 years of changing architectural styles. Shown here are the northern (top) and eastern blocks (bottom) facing the Square.

"Courthouse squares are such a uniquely American
public-place archetype that no survey would be complete without them."

From the panel discussion.

The 1880s Shelby County Courthouse, with its distinctive clock tower, still houses the county offices.

Public Buildings

Whether they be private or public, buildings define the urban environment and express the civic and cultural values of a community. The four buildings included here deliver on both counts. They were each conceived and designed with great public purpose in mind. On the outside they embellish their cities and on the inside they offer spectacular interior spaces that are thrilling to experience. They also represent the kind of civic institution (a library, two railroad stations, and a museum) where residents traditionally gather.

In a region that is characterized by its sprawl, the recently renovated and expanded Los Angeles Central Library makes an important statement about the civic value of maintaining a central public facility in downtown. New York City's Grand Central Terminal and Boston's South Station each provide an impressive port of entry to their cities. The Atrium of the Franklin Institute in Philadelphia, a modern addition to an old building, is a space that both embraces and involves the visiting public, particularly children. ∎

The Los Angeles Central Library.

Courtesy of the Los Angeles Central Library.

Los Angeles Central Library

Los Angeles, California

Office workers and schoolchildren break for lunch under the shade trees of the Maguire Garden.

The elaborately restored and expanded Los Angeles Central Library stands out among the modern glass skyscrapers, a boldly decorated Art Deco gem and a rare gesture of faith on the part of the city in its downtown. It narrowly escaped demolition. For years its fate hung in the balance as officials and citizens debated whether smaller libraries strewn throughout the region would not better serve the sprawling community. Its survival is due to a reaffirmation of the library's civic role.

Two fires at the Central Library in 1986, both set by arsonists, dramatized the state of the structure and reignited a thirty-year struggle to save the beautiful downtown landmark. In the end, a coalition of preservationists, government officials, and business leaders developed a plan to restore the building and add the space necessary to update its operations—all without adding to the density of the site or imposing a financial burden on the city. The key to the plan was selling the Library's air rights to two developers building nearby.

Today, restored in stunning detail, the Library is again a major cultural and civic presence in downtown Los Angeles. The reflecting pools ringed with palm trees in the library's original West Gardens had been sacrificed in the early 1960s to make room for yet another paved parking lot. They have now been restored to form the lush Maguire Garden, and a high-tech addition of more than 300,000 square feet—most of it underground—has more than doubled the size of the building. The result is a precious outdoor public space in a part of the city that is nearly devoid of such luxuries, and a focal center in an urban landscape that often seems to have none. ■

The Maguire Garden reproduces the Central Library's original formal entrance. Its reflecting pools are decorated with sculptures and glazed tiles inscribed with literary quotes in different languages. Branching paths lead to intimate side terraces.

A Complex Transaction

Beginning in the 1960s, various public agencies sought to either raze or sell Bertram Goodhue's beautiful 1926 Art Deco structure in order to build a larger, modern facility, but their proposals were either rejected by the voters or became bogged down in disputes. By the late 1970s, the city council had finally reached consensus on the idea of renovating and expanding the existing Library, however at just that time California's Proposition 13 reduced revenues severely and the plan was killed. The project lay dormant for the next five years until a study, backed by prominent downtown corporate leaders, came up with the strategy that would save the structure.

The solution, which cost the city nothing, was to sell the Library's air rights—the additional height allowed under current zoning but not utilized by the present building—to the developers of two buildings being erected on adjacent lots. After a series of complex transactions, that sale generated more than $125 million toward the Library's restoration. As part of the bargain, Maguire Thomas Partners, the developers of the two towers, constructed a 942-space underground parking garage and restored the Library's West Gardens.

Grand Terminals

Grand Central Terminal, Manhattan, New York
South Station, Boston, Massachusetts

I n addition to being magnificent examples of civic architecture that enrich the public environment, New York City's Grand Central Terminal and Boston's South Station have become engines of commerce. Once glamorous intercity terminals, they have successfully made the transition to everyday commuter stations by turning themselves into commercial centers—the equivalent of an old fashioned main street where commuters can run errands, eat, or window shop as they wait for their trains.

The renovation of Boston's historic South Station consolidated under one roof all intercity, commuter, bus, and subway lines.

In Boston, an $80 million renovation has given a new life to South Station, a neoclassical building on what was once the fringe of downtown but is now a district of office buildings. The Station has been rebuilt as a vital transportation hub serving both urban and interstate travelers, with Amtrak and commuter trains as well as a local metro line. The 300-foot-long main concourse has been transformed into a truly exciting indoor space, a street of kiosks and shops—dry cleaners, barbershops, newspaper stands, bookstores, bakeries—offering the kinds of services that were once widely available downtown but are now hard to find. Long neglected, and threatened with demolition in the 1970s, South Station has been reborn as an airy, pleasant place full of people and activity.

New York's Grand Central Terminal has been a major transportation center since it was built. In the 1960s, however, it was nearly gutted to make way

for a skyscraper. The drive to save it led to an important test of landmark legislation, a case taken clear to the Supreme Court. The terminal's majestic main concourse, 450 feet long, 160 feet wide, and 130 feet high, is possibly the greatest indoor public place in the country. It is a soaring space with spectacular top-to-bottom windows, a monumental staircase, and balconies beneath the frescoed ceiling that are a people-watching paradise. During the morning rush hours thousands of commuters enter the space from all four directions on two levels, swirl around the famous central clock, and spill out into the nearby streets in a tide that can be felt for blocks. Like South Station, Grand Central is in the process of redefining itself as a commuter hub. It is currently undergoing a complete interior renovation that will upgrade its shops and restaurants and even revive elements of the original plan, including a second monumental staircase on the east end of the concourse.

The public sector has been heavily involved in the refurbishment of these landmarks. New York State will provide a third of the estimated $114 million required to renovate Grand Central, while the Massachusetts Bay Transportation Authority helped

Transformed into a regional commuter hub, South Station has developed the patronage—a daily commuter flow of 36,000 by rail, 37,000 by subway, and 1,000 by bus—required to sustain itself commercially.

The 40,000-square-foot main concourse of Grand Central Terminal is lit by vast windows and clerestory lunettes in the frescoed vault, which depicts a Mediterranean night sky. Obscured by years of grime and soot, the ceiling is slated for restoration as part of the terminal's overall refurbishing.

underwrite the redesign of South Station. This is a dramatic reminder that trains—unlike cars—can help build cities. They have always been catalysts for real-estate development: the leasing of air rights over Grand Central's rail yards in 1934 led to the creation of Park Avenue and the construction of 17 office buildings and eight hotels. The recent restoration of South Station has spurred the construction of new office buildings nearby.

Train stations, with their unique ability to concentrate people and activities in one place, also nourish a sense of community. More than 50 special events are scheduled each year at South Station; the restored waiting rooms at Grand Central are also used for popular exhibits and concerts. These are public spaces that encourage people from all over the region to mingle. ■

"I now see the frescoed ceiling of the constellations in Grand Central Terminal as the only epic painting in New York—our Sistine Chapel."

George Negroponte, from his letter of nomination.

The café on the west balcony above Grand Central's main concourse is a good perch for people-watching.

A Landmark Decision

For one moment in the late 1970s, the future of landmark legislation for the entire nation hinged on a legal decision concerning Grand Central Terminal and the plans of its owners, Penn Central Railroad, to build a 55-story tower on top of it. The New York Landmarks Commission had rejected the tower scheme as "nothing more than an aesthetic joke...that would reduce the landmark itself to the status of a curiosity"—prompting Penn Central to take the city and the landmark law to court.

What was at issue was whether a preservation effort could benefit the public to such an extent as to justify its placing a burden on private property owners. After years of leasing and selling air rights over the terminal's rail yards, Penn Central had only one property left on which to build: the Terminal itself. Current zoning permitted the construction of 1.7 million square feet of office space on the site. Penn Central disputed the constitutionality of the landmark law, contending that it was taking away private property without just compensation.

In 1975, the court ruled in favor of Penn Central and thrust the law protecting individual landmarks into jeopardy. In response, the New York Municipal Arts Society orchestrated an extremely successful public-awareness campaign and assembled the Citizens Committee to Save Grand Central, to which Jacqueline Onassis lent her support and for which Madison Avenue developed the slogan, "No More Bites Out of the Big Apple."

After the Appellate Division overturned the original decision, unanimously upheld by the State Court of Appeals, the case then came before the United States Supreme Court. What had started as a local issue had become a national one, as every preservation law in the country now stood to lose. The Sierra Club, the National Trust for Historic Preservation, the states of New York and California, and the City Bar Association joined in the amicus brief. In 1978, the Supreme Court upheld the landmarks law, in a 6-3 decision written by Justice William Brennan.

An exhibition of artist Red Grooms's sculptures depicting famous Manhattan landmarks, such as the Woolworth Building, celebrated the reopening of Grand Central's main waiting room.

Photo by Frank English. Courtesy of Metro-North Commuter Railroad.

125

The Atrium

Franklin Institute, Philadelphia, Pennsylvania

The Atrium of the Franklin Institute in Philadelphia, part of an addition completed in 1990, is an indoor town square for the thousands of children who visit the museum's science exhibits. Designed in primary colors, with skylights, playful columns, and fanciful light fixtures, the Atrium has given this venerable institution a new vitality. Children roam the bright space, running up and down the circular ramps and calling to each other from the metal bridges that bisect the space. Visitors, volunteers, staff, and casual passersby—access to the Atrium is free of charge—drift through the space, lending it a diverse and bustling urbanity. A small café and amphitheater, often used for lectures and shows, add to its appeal as a public facility.

A dramatic display for an upcoming exhibit, "The Dinosaurs of Jurassic Park," includes a full-scale Tyrannosaurus Rex.

At any given time, but particularly in winter and on rainy afternoons, the Atrium is filled with young people—raising the intriguing possibility that this exciting public space with its invitation to learning is considered a viable alternative to the sorts of places they might otherwise tend to congregate in: private indoor playgrounds, game rooms, amusement parks, and enclosed shopping malls. ∎

The Atrium ramps connect to the bridges and balconies of the Mandell Center, the Franklin Institute's new wing devoted to special exhibitions and containing the domed Imax theater.

"What does a family do on a Saturday morning when they want to take their kids away from the VCR, the television, and the computer? Right now the solution in the suburbs is they can go to the mall, they can go to the Discovery Zone—a paid indoor playground—they can have lunch in a fast-food restaurant. It is a basic question vexing everyone, and one that the Atrium begins to answer."

From the panel discussion.

The Atrium's curvilinear shape is echoed by the quirky light fixtures. The space connects the new wing to the older sections of the museum, but invites visitors to linger.

Farmers' Markets

Farmers' markets began to decline in the 1940s, slowly pushed aside by the arrival of the refrigerator, the invention of cellophane for wrapping, and the rise of interstate trucking —innovations that made possible the development of supermarkets. But they did not die out altogether, as the places in this chapter illustrate.

Seattle's Pike Place Market, thanks to significant community pressure, is perhaps the best-known example of a farmers' market that has survived the test of time. This rambling aggregate of warehouses and sheds crammed with hundreds of shops is credited with having financially turned around a large area of the city. Likewise, Market Square, in Roanoke, Virginia, an old but decrepit market, became the flagship project in the transformation of a turn-of-the-century historic district into a shopping and cultural area. The stability of the Central Market in Lancaster, Pennsylvania, the country's oldest farmers' market, has never been in question. Established in 1730, it is supported by both the city and citizens of Lancaster, who recognize its economic and cultural importance. Finally, there is the Italian Market in South Philadelphia, a big raucous market whose authenticity seems to defy local health and fire codes. It serves the city's diverse ethnic population and delivers all the mercurial thrills of a true marketplace. ■

The main entrance to Pike Place Market, in Seattle.

Pike Place Market

Seattle, Washington

Although it is housed in a haphazard accumulation of old brick, concrete, and timber warehouses and sheds, Seattle's Pike Place Market, the site of a farmers' market since 1907, is one of the liveliest, most appealing public locales in the country. A visually anarchic and socially tolerant place, the market is an extraordinary multilevel maze of passageways, arcades, streets, stairs, and balconies, in which signs direct the visitor to go up, down, right, left, behind, and beyond. The buildings, each in a different stage of renovation or decay, are crammed with hundreds of small to minuscule shops selling an incredible range of goods.

Although the farmers' market and the fish market are only a small part of the whole complex, they are the soul of Pike Place. The market begins at daybreak, when the flower and produce vendors, who rent tables on a daily basis, arrive. In short order, the empty sheds are loaded with colorful seasonal produce, sculptures of dramatically piled crabs and salmons, and other fish and seafood. Soon after, the crowds begin to build; desirables— residents, tourists, artists, musicians, merchants, the elderly, children—and undesirables alike mingle at the market until late in the evening.

Very few places in the nation accommodate such a wide range of activities and people as Pike Place, and this diversity is exactly what citizens were trying to preserve when they objected to turning Pike Place into a picturesque gaslight historic district. Properties were intentionally kept small, and leases were given only to shop owners who would be on the premises—

Top: Small growers selling flowers and fresh fruit keep the farmers' market alive at Pike Place. The tradition dates from 1907, when the city established a market here. Thousands were said to have waited at dawn to cheer the farmers who came that first day. Bottom: Fruits and vegetable are piled high over empty crates, in the traditional fashion of public markets.

Dramatic sculptures made of salmon and crab decorate the fish stalls.

a move that has effectively kept retail chains out of the market and led to its seemingly impromptu mix of stores.

Still, because of its success (Pike Place has operated in its current incarnation for twenty-five years), very few people realize how fragile the market's economy is. And even fewer are aware that one of the market's most remarkable qualities—the unadulterated urban experience it offers—is equally precarious. The pressure to loosen renting restrictions and let in the big retailers has escalated in the past decade as these large establishments have begun to open facilities in successful downtown districts, such as Pike Place. Should the renting and ownership restrictions be relaxed, the market's quirky mix of stores would be quickly eroded, and residents could lose one of the defining venues of their city. ∎

"Outdated, Unprofitable, Inefficient..."

Set in downtown Seattle, on a hill overlooking Puget Sound, Pike Place Market has been the site of a popular farmers' market for nearly 90 years. In the 1960s, however, the badly deteriorated market was declared "outdated, unprofitable, and inefficient" by the powers that be and slated for urban renewal. Led by local architect Victor Steinbrueck, Seattle citizens organized Friends of the Market and gathered fifty-thousand signatures for a petition to declare the market a protected historic district. The issue was put on the city ballot (though not before the district was reduced to a tenth of its original size), and in 1971, despite opposition from both daily newspapers, citizens voted decisively to protect the market.

Three Farmers' Markets

Central Market, Lancaster, Pennsylvania
Market Square, Roanoke, Virginia
Italian Market, Philadelphia, Pennsylvania

The Lancaster Central Market, the Roanoke Market Square, and the Philadelphia Italian Market are three variations on the farmers' market, an institution as old as the city itself. In addition to

bringing fresh food grown in the immediate countryside into the heart of a community, these adaptable public facilities can light up and energize whole districts of a city, attracting residents without the need for commercial gimmicks or complex marketing formulas. All three of the examples here—the venerable Lancaster Central Market, the big boisterous Italian Market, and historic Market Square—are vigorous commercial facilities that inject their cities with an energy, once taken for granted, that has now disappeared from most communities.

Central Market, located on the same site in

The Central Market, at the corner of King and Queen Streets in downtown Lancaster, is housed in a solidly built Romanesque building maintained by the city (top). Modern refrigeration cases have made their way into the 250-year-old Central Market, expanding the range of products sold there.

Lancaster since 1730, harkens back to a time when the farmers' market was a community's most important venue. The oldest continuously operating public market in the country, it is a place where traditions have been kept alive. Its central location, long history, and beautiful redbrick Romanesque building, constructed by the city in 1889, have made

Commercial interactions at Market Square often cross over into friendship as shoppers and farmers get to know each other.

Design '79

Market Square and its surrounding district were renovated as the direct result of an intensive citizen-involvement process called Design '79. Initiated by Bern Ewert, Roanqke's progressive city manager, in an effort to build consensus on the future of the community, the program involved asking citizens for their ideas on how the city could attract some of the millions of tourists visiting the Blue Ridge Mountains while also preserving the community's historic fabric and protecting its traditions. Ewart opened a storefront in downtown Roanoke and invited passersby to drop in and offer suggestions. Citizens were also encouraged to share their ideas with architects and planners during four televised town meetings.

One of the most important suggestions generated by the five-month program was to improve the historic farmers' market and renovate and convert an adjoining warehouse into a cultural center. Within three years of Design '79's conclusion, Roanoke's residents voted in favor of bond issues to pay for 52 projects (all of which originated with the program) in a total investment of $17 million in public funds and $47 million in private ones.

a visit to the market a chief ritual in the life of this city. Every Tuesday, Friday, and Saturday, members of the region's Amish community and other stall holders arrive early in the morning to unpack and display their products. Shortly thereafter, a trickle of early-morning shoppers—old people, mothers with children, restaurant chefs—begins to arrive, and by lunchtime, when office workers pour into the market, the crowd is at its peak.

Market Square, the site of a farmers' market for more than a hundred years, has become an institution of another kind for the city of Roanoke. Back in the late 1970s, this turn-of-the-century commercial district was thought to have no future, but as a result of its humble farmers' market's success, it has become the keystone of a new cultural and shopping district and a catalyst in downtown Roanoke's revitalization. Open every day from early morning until dusk, and sometimes until late in the evening, the outdoor farmers' market is set up in the square and along the two-block Market Street, providing a constant flow of people to what

The mix of history, culture, and fresh vegetables at Market Square in Roanoke has proven to be the right recipe for luring residents back downtown; it has also induced visitors to the outlying Blue Ridge Mountains to spend time in the city.

Photo by Daniel T. Seginak.

Fruits and vegetables are just a small part of what is available for sale at the Italian Market in Philadelphia. Secondhand records, clothing, toys, utensils, watches, and small electronic devices are a few of the many items sold there.

has become Roanoke's most significant public place. The 1922 Market Building, which once housed wholesale produce operations, has been transformed into an international food court, while a warehouse across the street has been renovated as a cultural center containing science, art, and history museums and a theater. In addition, various historic buildings accommodating offices and small shops have been renovated.

Building codes, sanitary codes, and traffic regulations all seem to have been forgotten at South Philadelphia's Italian Market, a noisy chaotic city market that serves the many ethnic neighborhoods of the city, offering fresh produce and an impressive array of meats, fish, and prepared foods seven days a week. It stretches along seven blocks of Ninth Avenue (from Wharton to Christian streets) in the Italian section of Philadelphia, and more than 250 stores and as many more side-by-side stalls face each other along the incredibly narrow, crowded sidewalk. The street behind is filled with chest-high piles of cardboard boxes and wooden crates, burned right in the street (a convenient source of heat in winter). Surrounded by the sights, sounds, and smells of Ninth Avenue in all its messy variety, a walk through this farmers' market is an extraordinary experience—one that has been mostly cleaned up and toned down everywhere else. ■

Photo by Daniel T. Seginak.

Markets laid out like the one in Philadelphia used to be more common in cities. The fruit and vegetable stalls on the sidewalks faced bakeries and fish, meat, and general food stores—which together offered a full array of food products within a few blocks.

The Market Master

The Market Master is the traditional title of Central Market's manager, the person appointed by Lancaster's mayor to be responsible for everything from opening the doors in the wee hours of the morning to settling disputes between stand holders and customers, examining the produce for quality, and coaching the volunteer band that entertains shoppers at lunchtime. This 250-year-old tradition is strongly supported by the city government, which realizes the economic and cultural value of the market.

Photo by Daniel T. Seginak.

Despite the precarious building conditions, the crowds, the babel of languages, and the total disregard for aesthetics (except, of course, in the fruit and produce displays), the Italian Market is the place that best shows Philadelphia's rich ethnic diversity.

Photo by Daniel T. Seginak.

Many of the stores in the Italian market have been in the same families for decades.

Turning Points

At the time they were created, each of the places in this chapter represented a daring break with contemporary practices. All of them have gone on to become the yardstick against which similar projects are measured. The first of them, a dramatic—and quintessentially American—space, is the Lawn at the University of Virginia. Here Thomas Jefferson realized his revolutionary ideas about education and society in creating an open, democratic institution of learning in stark contrast to the authoritarian educational ideas of the time. A century after their conception and design, New York's magnificent Central Park and Prospect Park and San Francisco's Golden Gate Park still provide a green escape for the urban masses, exemplifying the inspiration and foresight of their chief builders, Frederick Law Olmsted, Calvert Vaux, William Hammond Hall, and John McLaren. When it was first unveiled, the Vietnam Veterans Memorial stirred up a highly divisive controversy, yet over time its simple, modern design has subdued the turmoil. Finally, Oriole Park at Camden Yards has returned a great American public institution—the ballpark —to the heart of the city, demonstrating that even a stadium facility can be integrated into the complex fabric of a downtown area. ■

The Vietnam Veterans Memorial.

The Lawn

University of Virginia, Charlottesville, Virginia

A hundred and seventy years after its completion, the Lawn at the University of Virginia functions much as its architect, Thomas Jefferson, envisioned it; students and faculty still live side by side in the academic village that is centered on a public place rich with opportunities for informal learning. Jefferson's concept, which revolutionized the American campus and influenced the lives of thousands of students, embodied the egalitarian values of the country's budding democracy and rejected the authoritarian educational ideas of the time.

The simplicity of the Lawn's layout is integral to its great beauty and powerful urbanism. Bordering two sides of the gently sloping green are white

In a time when buildings of historic significance are often converted for private or commercial use, it is remarkable that students and faculty still live on the Lawn, just as they did in 1826.

colonnades uniting two-story faculty pavilions (containing living quarters and classrooms) with one-story student rooms. A third side is enclosed by the steps and terrace of the Rotunda, which, together with the colonnades, once framed an unobstructed southern view of the hills of 19th-century Virginia. But three buildings by McKim, Mead & White, erected in 1899, have since sealed off this vista, adding an element of monumentality never intended by the plan.

Jefferson's creation is not a grand or formal place —the colonnades are modest in size, and the Rotunda, which provides the university's architectural focus, is a building of unadorned classicism. To compare the Lawn with the more elaborate public places of Europe, as people often do, is superficial and unnecessary. It is an original and intrinsically American place, shaped, in the words of the person who nominated it, "by the very idea of American democracy." ∎

A Heathen University

Jefferson's design, which made the Rotunda library the university's aesthetic and spiritual focus, was a radical departure from tradition. From the beginning his secular institution offended local clerics: the omission of a chapel from among the important buildings facing the Lawn set off a controversy that would not be laid to rest until after Jefferson's death. Eventually, a small Gothic chapel was erected in a location off the Lawn, and the secular sanctity of the University was preserved.

The Lawn is a convenient outdoor forum in which students and faculty can share thoughts and ideas, as well as a place for just relaxing.

The colonnades serve as a front porch for the student rooms; messages pinned on doors, stacks of firewood, and the sound of music are evidence of this cherished landmark's human and accessible character.

Grand Parks

Golden Gate Park, San Francisco, California
Central Park, Manhattan, New York
Prospect Park, Brooklyn, New York

*New Yorkers in Central Park's grassy
Sheep Meadow escape the heat.*

Central Park and Prospect Park, in New York, and Golden Gate Park, in San Francisco, belong to a handful of public parks across America that are notable for the bold social and civic vision and inspired design that led to their creation. Built more than a century ago, beginning in 1858, they are now central to the large metropolitan areas they serve, and the biggest threat to their survival is the constant wear and tear of everyday use.

The creation of the parks marked the beginning of a new era in American city planning. In response to increasingly unhealthy and overcrowded conditions, civic leaders and planners built new public preserves that offered greater access to both natural resources —grass, trees, fresh air—and recreational opportunities. In just thirty years they drastically changed the shape of American cities, establishing

A view of the Park looking south toward 59th Street. Central Park hardly deserved its name when it was first built. At the time, Manhattan barely extended north beyond 40th Street.

The Central Park Conservancy

The Central Park Conservancy, created by Mayor Ed Koch in 1980, has been wildly successful in raising money for Central Park. Fifty thousand private donors, corporations, and foundations supply more than half the Park's annual operating budget, half the funding for capital improvements and Park personnel, and most of the funding for recreational programming.

The financial success of the Conservancy has cast a shadow of privatization over this most public of public places. While complaints about increased regulations, tighter controls, and the gentrification of some of the park's facilities may be justified, they seem more than balanced out by the unprecedented physical renaissance of the park and the fact that millions of New Yorkers of all classes continue to enjoy its facilities. The Conservancy is well on its way toward realizing its goal of completely restoring the Park's landscape and facilities by the year 2000. Far from being a threat, the merging of public and private resources appears to be the only way to preserve such a priceless asset as Central Park.

some of the first democratic spaces specifically conceived to be shared by people of different races, ethnic backgrounds, and social and economic classes.

The plans of the parks are unsurpassed models of public space design. As William H. Whyte, noted author and longtime observer of cities, has often remarked, "The genius of Central Park is that it is a big place that is intimate in the workings of its small pieces." The same can be said of Prospect Park and Golden Gate Park. Each day, the parks are virtually reconfigured to mirror the needs of the thousands of people who arrive knowing that they will find a place, even an audience, for whatever they may want to do. This ability to change, to accommodate many different people and uses, is what makes these parks the most important places in their respective cities.

The extraordinary popularity of the parks (last year Central Park was visited by 15 million people,

A violinist performs by the Conservatory Water in Central Park. Olmsted intended Central Park to provide relief from "the confinement, bustle and monotonous street division of the city," and to restore a sense of mystery to the lives of city dwellers.

The 1,023 acres designated for Golden Gate Park were located far from the city center, on a barren expanse of sand known as the Outside Lands. When asked his opinion of the site, in 1866, Frederick Law Olmsted commented that it would be unwise to assume "that trees which would delight the eye could be made to grow" there.

Prospect Park by 6 million and Golden Gate Park by an astounding 20 million) has taken a toll. By the end of the 1970s, signs of decline and outright neglect were visible everywhere. At the same time, the public sector lacked the funds to maintain, let alone restore such large parks. The problem was particularly acute in Central and Prospect parks.

In 1980, the Central Park Conservancy was created to undertake a massive restoration of the Park. A similar organization, the Alliance, was created for Prospect Park. Both entities, which are also responsible for maintaining the parks, are not-for-profit organizations funded by private contributions. Although they have been criticized as part of a trend toward the privatization of New York's most important parks, their impact has been extraordinary. Private contributions have also played a role in the refurbishment of Golden Gate Park, although through the San Francisco Department of

The San Francisco Model Yacht Club holds weekend regattas from March through November at Spreckels Lake. Competitors sometimes include flocks of migratory birds.

Parks and Recreation. Central Park, Prospect Park, and Golden Gate Park today are immensely improved places, cleaner, safer, and more beautiful than ever. ∎

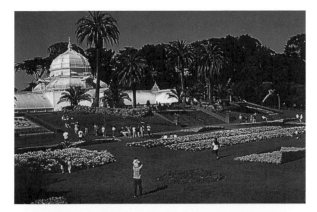

Golden Gate Park's oldest building, the glass-paneled Victorian Conservatory of Flowers, is in a flower-filled valley at the northeast corner.

Although the Prospect Park Alliance has done much to restore and maintain the park, its budget is just a twentieth of the Central Park Conservancy's, due to the difference in the boroughs' economic bases and real-estate values. To compensate, the Alliance has developed one of the most extensive volunteer programs in the country, in which unpaid workers log in an estimated 20,000 hours per year.

In many ways, Olmsted and Vaux considered their design for Central Park a preparatory exercise for Prospect Park. The more compact site of Brooklyn's park for the people lent itself to a better balance of meadow, lake, and forest and allowed for a more complete separation of pedestrian paths and roadways, so that a few steps into the park one loses awareness of the surrounding city.

Vietnam Veterans Memorial

Washington, D.C.

The polished black granite wings of the Vietnam Veterans Memorial descend gently beneath the level of the Washington Mall, creating an intensely private place of remembrance and mourning. Stark, subdued, supremely modern in its design, the memorial is in sharp contrast to the other celebratory monuments of the Mall. Its only decorative element is the listing of more than 57,000 war dead inscribed on its two retaining walls aligned with the Lincoln Memorial and the Washington Monument. The names of the fallen are not arranged in alphabetical order or according to military branch, unit, or rank, but simply follow, one by one, in roughly chronological order according to the year of their death. This way they do not glorify the abstract hierarchy of war, but rather thrust the visitor into the personal reality of those who died.

In the past fourteen years, the privately funded

Vietnam Veterans Memorial has become the Capital's most visited monument. More than two million people a year visit the Memorial, a peaceful spot that embraces equally those who come to honor a friend or relative and those who come just to look. It is perhaps the monument's lack of rhetoric, its refusal to praise or condemn the institutional nature of war, that has enabled this beautiful piece of public sculpture to succeed where others have failed. It has united those who supported the war and those who opposed it, and become a place of national healing. ∎

A Divisive Issue

The Vietnam Veterans Memorial, conceived by veterans and paid for with private donations, has a unique place among the government-sponsored public monuments on Washington's Mall. Completed in 1982, it was the idea of Jan Scruggs, a veteran who returned from Vietnam in 1969. Ten years later, he established the Vietnam Veterans Memorial Fund with a small group of veterans, and enlisted the help of Charles Matthias, a Republican senator from Maryland. Matthias led a campaign in Congress to allocate land for the monument.

A national competition was held to select a design. Out of 1,400 anonymous entries, the jury unanimously selected the work of a twenty-two year old Chinese-American architecture student from Yale University, Maya Ying Lin. Her non-traditional design angered a small group of veterans within the Fund, and suddenly the Memorial became a divisive issue. Finally, the artist Frederick Hart was commissioned to create another, traditional sculpture. His bronze of three infantrymen was placed in a nearby grove.

Many of the visitors trace the names of lost friends or relatives on paper, adding an interactive dimension to a visit (above) or leave gifts of letters, flowers, and personal tokens at the foot of the memorial (below). At last count 48,000 of them had been collected.

Oriole Park
at Camden Yards

Baltimore, Maryland

O riole Park, a state-of-the-art ballpark built in the thick of Baltimore's residential neighborhoods, has radically changed the way cities design and locate stadiums, usually relegated to the outskirts or suburbs. Situated in Camden Yards, an old railway and manufacturing district a few blocks west of the bustling Inner Harbor, the park is respectful of the style and scale of its setting and incorporates several existing historic buildings. Near-capacity attendance, achieved each year since the stadium's opening in 1992, quickly dispelled any concerns about placing the facility so close to downtown. In fact, despite the Orioles' lackluster 1995 season, the park had the second-largest home attendance of all major league ballparks, with nearly 43,000 people attending each game.

From the street, Oriole Park resembles a small, early 1900s stadium, with steel trusses, an arched brick facade, and a sun roof sloping over the upper deck. Inside, however, are all the technical advantages of a modern ballpark: a sophisticated drainage system under the natural grass turf reduces the chance of rainouts; a thousand loudspeakers distributed throughout the facility provide distortion-free sound; and a glare-resistant lighting system illuminates the stands. To prevent the stadium from towering over its neighbors, the field is sunk 16 feet below street level; instead of climbing, half of the spectators entering Oriole Park walk comfortably to their seats.

By design, fans literally walk away at the end of each game and disperse through the neighborhood to

Oriole Park is the forerunner of a new generation of stadiums built in a close relationship with their cities. The Baltimore skyline is visible through the gap in center field: a visual reminder that the ballpark is an extension of the city. The former freight facility of the B & O Railway Company (opposite), seen over right field, has been renovated to provide office space for the Orioles. The old warehouse facade reinforces the park's historical and architectural context.

use the buses, light rail, Metro, and commuter lines that connect the park to the region, for there is minimal on-site parking. This has not only minimized congestion, but has increased the foot traffic and exposure of surrounding businesses. Studies made by the State of Maryland estimate that the Orioles generate $100 million annually in economic activity in and around Camden Yards; bars and restaurants stay open late, a local hotel has doubled its number of rooms, even the Convention Center, located nearby, has boosted its bookings and plans an expansion.

It cost the State, which funded the stadium almost entirely through the sale of taxable and tax-exempt revenue bonds, $300 million to build Oriole Park. The debt service on the bonds is paid through revenues from a special instant scratch-card lottery and from profits from the rental of the facility—close to $10 million a year.

Oriole Park has created an unexpected new attraction for downtown, and demonstrated that a stadium can be added to the list of civic structures that contribute to the appearance, economic well-being, and social life of a community. It has added to the complex mix of the Inner Harbor area as well, already a place of many uses. And yes, Oriole Park is a terrific place to watch baseball, with its bright green grass and view of the Baltimore skyline. ■

Park City

The decision to limit on-site parking at Oriole Park and strengthen its public transportation links shows the bold thinking of the developers. Since the urban location of the park precluded the creation of the customary ocean-sized parking lots surrounding most sports facilities—which go unused most of the time—only a fifth of the 25,000 parking spaces created were located at the stadium; the rest were scattered through the surrounding neighborhoods.

The need to look for parking forces families from the Baltimore Beltway and beyond to drive into town and walk through the downtown neighborhoods to the ballpark. As a result, many end up staying in the city after dark to eat, stroll, or shop at the Inner Harbor—and in the process become reacquainted with the city's downtown core.

Afterword:
The Search Is On

By Tony Hiss

With one superb bouquet in hand, the Search for Great American Public Places needs to keep blossoming, riotously. It seems more than likely that this country has at least 60,000 public places that enrich our community, focus our regions, and consecrate our nation. This collection of 60 magnificent and mostly flourishing examples will probably wind up, East-Coast heavy though it is, as the foreword, the appetizer, the trailer, the manifesto for a desperately needed comprehensive national survey.

But whatever the number, it's probably too small. Five-sixths of the places celebrated in this book were built before 1950, and since then the United States population has grown by two-thirds. By the year 2025, there may be 361 million Americans, more than double our numbers at the end of World War II. Thirty years gives us ample time to build hundreds of millions of TV sets and computers to opulently furnish the virtual worlds of those future Americans. But what about their real-life surroundings?

The first thing any search needs is its searchers, and a portable book can be a powerfully reinforcing, if slightly disguised, recruiting tool. Now that you're reading this page—even if you just picked up the book idly, and happened to start flipping through it backwards—you have been found.

What an unbelievably, if unfairly, unfashionable topic we have all taken on. "Public," a word almost everybody once liked the ring of, went into free fall during the anti-egalitarian eighties, before bottoming out in our own downsizing decade as a sour substitute for "second-rate." (Quick—how much fun do you automatically associate with any of the following: public housing, public transportation, public assistance, public service, public rest rooms, public relations, public-address systems.)

And what a complex, tricky job awaits us. So short

The Dana Center at the Harlem Meer.

Courtesy of Central Park Conservancy.

Bicycles are increasingly becoming the vehicle of choice for getting around congested cities.

as it is, this fearlessly inclusive book stretches our understanding of the word "place" beyond all previous bounds, so that it now encompasses such things as the act of climbing upstairs (the Low Library Steps, in New York); or a thin line arcing across the Eastern wilderness (the 13-state, 2,100-mile-long Appalachian National Scenic Trail, which runs from mountaintop to mountaintop between Maine and Georgia); or even a series of objects moving in different directions (streetcars grinding through New Orleans, and ferryboats bobbing about on San Francisco Bay).

My hunch is that the Search for Great American Public Places, as it unfolds, won't be a kind of "Where's Waldo?" treasure hunt, because suddenly we'll be far too busy putting together recovery programs that can get exhausted public places back on their feet. Governments are cutting back, and corporations are strapped, but the places that are calling out to us are daring us to be ingenious:

- In New York, thanks to a deal brokered by the city's Housing and Preservation Department, part of the profits from a nearby parking lot help pay for the upkeep of Washington Market Park, a small, elegant, community-managed park way downtown in Manhattan so beloved by its neighbors that every summer it's almost overrun by picnickers, ballplayers, gardeners, sketchers, jungle-gym climbers, and, occasionally, wedding parties.

- After a disastrous oil spill in New York harbor, five local governments agreed to funnel some of the fines they collected to a small group of ecologists from the New York City Parks and Recreation Department's Natural Resources Group, who then showed 1,000 eager volunteers, ranging from high-school students to senior citizens, how to heal a wild shorefront park, as befouled as a Kuwaiti oil field, by hand-planting and hand-fertilizing a quarter of a million native marsh-grass seedlings. This Staten Island recovery program has been so successful that it's now the model for cleaning up off-shore oil spills in the United States.

In public places, people of all sorts are welcomed and encouraged to linger, and minds of all kinds may

freely congregate. And have fun. And even evolve: the California historian Gunther Barth showed fifteen years ago, in his book *City People* how 19th-century rural Americans gathered strength not so much by moving into cities as by thronging to the new public and semipublic places those cities had just invented. There were apartment houses, which taught people how to live together; department stores, which brought more people downtown; baseball parks, which gave free instruction in teamwork; and vaudeville houses, which let people laugh at themselves.

The outdoor café at Boston's Post Office Square, which sits on top of a seven-story underground garage.

It is our minds that might be weakened by the destruction and degradation of great public places. Too many of our surviving public treasures need replenishing, and this book is telling us how to rescue them. Public places live by being loved. And to stay loved, they need to be lovable, which means that, like Tinkerbell, they can only be revived by people who believe in them, who care enough to start taking care of just a piece of them. But, even before that, we have to embrace them as places.

Take Fifth Avenue, in New York City, Manhattan's Main Street, seven miles long and one of the best-known streets in the world. It's the official dividing line between East Side and West Side. But although it borders two of the places celebrated in the book—Central Park and Rockefeller Center—and is only a short distance away from two more—Grand Central Terminal and Bryant Park—it has languished for

Initially designed for the automobile, Country Club Plaza, in Kansas City, Missouri, has become a pedestrian-friendly place, now that it no longer sits alone, as it originally did, in the middle of a Kansas cornfield.

years, because everyone thinks of it as a corridor, and no one—at least for the last 40 years, during the time I've lived a block away from it—treats it as a place. Fifth Avenue passes through Harlem, and alongside the Gold Coast apartment houses next to Central Park; it links midtown Manhattan's department stores and office towers, and anchors Greenwich Village. And none of these estranged neighborhoods have recognized that it is the common ground they should take care of together.

Forty years ago, before its placeness was misplaced, Fifth Avenue, then a two-way street, had double-decker buses, which invited you to float above the traffic. Many different pairs of eyes could focus on two floors of the street at once—so the bottom twenty feet of everything had to stay scrubbed, not just the bottom ten feet. Jane Jacobs has since taught us about how streets stay alive when eyes are constantly focussed on them.

Forty years ago, Fifth Avenue had (of all things!) the most beautiful stoplights in the world—bronze, diminutive, delicately molded, surmounted by tiny statues of the winged Mercury. Unique. All gone.

Children need places like this fountain in Post Office Square, Boston, which gives them an opportunity for play while sharing the space with adults.

Why? These lights only flashed red and green, and the city shifted to red, yellow, and green lights. The old lights could have survived, with a bit of reconfiguring, if Fifth had registered in people's minds as a place—you only had to slice them open between the red and green lights and fashion a new bit that held yellow lights. More expensive? Yes, but Fifth Avenue building owners, who have in the last few years banded together to pay for improvements, just as building owners around Bryant Park did a few years earlier, would have been happy to save the lights in order to burnish New York and enhance the value of their property.

Now that we have placeness back in our heads, the inclusive solution won't be to bring Mercury back just to Fifth Avenue—the challenge, far broader, is to start making other streets distinctive and worthy of the gods, to "build as if place mattered," as Scott Bernstein, of Chicago's Center for Neighborhood Technology, likes to say.

Welcome to a team searching for itself. Together, we may have a chance to rediscover, recover, and raise up the great public places of the 21st-century America. ∎

Getting There

For the reader's convenience the 60 places are here arranged by State.

Appalachian National Scenic Trail passes through the states of Connecticut, Georgia, Maine, Maryland, Massachusetts, New Hampshire, New Jersey, New York, North Carolina, Pennsylvania, Tennessee, Vermont, Virginia and West Virginia

California
Los Angeles
    El Pueblo de Los Angeles
    Los Angeles Central Library
    Union Station
San Francisco
    Golden Gate Park
    Golden Gate National
        Recreation Area
    Grace Marchant Garden
    San Francisco Bay Ferries
    Washington Square
Venice
    Oceanfront Walk

Connecticut
New Haven
    The Green

Florida
Miami Beach
    Ocean Drive
Seaside

Indiana
Madison
    Main Street
New Harmony

Louisiana
New Orleans
    The French Quarter
    St. Charles Avenue Streetcars

Maryland
Baltimore
    Oriole Park at Camden Yards

Massachusetts
Boston
    Faneuil Hall Marketplace
    Newbury Street
    Post Office Square
    South Station
Nantucket

Mississippi
Oxford
    Courthouse Square

Missouri
Kansas City
    Country Club Plaza

New Hampshire
Portsmouth

New Jersey
Camden
    Yorkship Village

New Mexico
Acoma and Taos
Santa Fe
    The Plaza

New York
Greenwich
Brooklyn
    Brooklyn Bridge
        Promenade
    Coney Island
    Jacob Riis Park
    Prospect Park
Manhattan
    Battery Park City
    Esplanade
    Bryant Park
    Central Park
    Columbia University
        Low Memorial Library
            Steps
    Grand Central Terminal
    Rockefeller Center
        The Promenade and
            Plaza
    Times Square

    Union Square Market
    West Side Community
        Garden
Queens
    Socrates Sculpture Park

North Carolina
Blue Ridge Parkway

Ohio
Sidney
    Courthouse Square
Yellow Springs
    Xenia Avenue

Oregon
Ashland
    Lithia Park
Portland
    Pioneer Courthouse Square

Pennsylvania
Lancaster
    Central Market
Philadelphia
    Franklin Institute
        The Atrium
    Italian Market

South Carolina
Charleston

Tennessee
Chattanooga
    Riverwalk

Virginia
Blue Ridge Parkway
Charlottesville
    The Lawn, University of
        Virginia
Norfolk
    Diggs Town
Roanoke
    Market Square

Washington
Seattle
    Pike Place Market

Washington, D.C.
Vietnam Veterans Memorial

Coney Island Boardwalk.

Photo by Matt Longo.

Some Readings

Visions

Grace Marchant Garden, San Francisco, California

"Let's Save This 'State of Grace.'" *San Francisco Examiner*, February 23, 1986.

"Donation Drive Saves Marchant Garden Plot." *San Francisco Examiner*, April 10, 1986.

"Saving Grace's Garden." *The Trust for Public Land Update*, No. 16, Summer, 1986.

Randolph Delehanty, *San Francisco*. New York: Dial Press, 1988.

Randolph Delehanty, *San Francisco: the Ultimate Guide*. San Francisco: Chronicle Books, 1989.

Socrates Sculpture Park, Queens, New York

"Best of Manhattan '93: Best Alternative Gallery." *New York Press*, September 15-21, 1993.

Dennis Hevesi, "Sculpture Garden Rises in a New Patch of Green." *The New York Times*, May 26, 1994.

Kathleen Sampey, "Art Park Grows on Waterfront." *Daily News*, May 26, 1994.

Diana Mosher, "Socrates Sculpture Park a Hit with Adults and Kids in L.I.C." *Queens Chronicle Magazine*, August 12, 1994.

The West Side Community Garden, Manhattan, New York

Lynden B. Miller, "Perennials in American Gardens." *The Garden Journal of the Royal Horticultural Society*, Vol. 111, Part 8, August 1986.

The Trust for Public Land. *Information Exchange*, Fall, 1988.

Joyce Young, "West Side in Bloom." *Daily News*, April 28, 1989.

Bernice Kanner, "Friends of the Earth." *New York*, January 15, 1990.

Connections

Golden Gate National Recreation Area, San Francisco, California

Margot Patterson Doss, *San Francisco at Your Feet*. New York: Grove Press, Inc., 1974.

Jane Futcher, *Marin, The Place, The People*. New York: Holt, Reinhart and Winston, 1981.

"Interview: Brian O'Neill's Golden Opportunity." *Land and People*, Vol. 6, No. 1, Spring 1994.

Lithia Park, Ashland, Oregon

O'Harra, Marjorie, *Lithia Park*. Ashland, Oregon: Ashland Parks and Recreation Department, 1994.

Appalachian National Scenic Trail

Benton Mackaye. Foreword to Ronald M. Fisher, *The Appalachian Trail*. Washington, D.C.: National Geographic Society, 1972.

Ronald Foresta, "Transformation of the Appalachian Trail." *Geographical Review*, Vol. 77, No. 1, 1987.

Charles H. W. Foster, *The Appalachian National Scenic Trail: A Time to be Bold*. Harpers Ferry, West Virginia: Appalachian Trail Conference, 1987.

Union Square Market, Manhattan, New York

Laura Van Tuyl, "Union Square Greenmarket: Rural Bounty in Manhattan." *The Christian Science Monitor*, September 26, 1991.

Margaret White Van Buren, "The Catskill Connection." *Catskill Center News*, Fall 1992.

Marian Burros, "His Urban Harvest." *The New York Times*, October 3, 1993.

Molly O'Neill, "A City's Dreams Go to Market." *The New York Times*, August 17, 1994.

Pleasurable Rides

St. Charles Avenue Streetcars, New Orleans, Louisiana

The New Orleans Chapter of the American Institute of Architects, *A Guide to New Orleans Architecture*. New Orleans: American Institute of Architects, 1974.

San Francisco Bay Ferries, San Francisco, California

Margot Patterson Doss, *San Francisco at Your Feet*. New York: Grove Press, Inc., 1974.

Sarah Bird Wright, *Ferries of America*. Atlanta, Georgia: Peachtree Publishers, 1987.

Brooklyn Bridge Promenade, Brooklyn, New York

David G. McCullough, *The Great Bridge*. New York: Simon and Schuster, 1972.

Alan Trachtenberg, *Brooklyn Bridge*. Chicago: University of Chicago Press, 1979.

Union Station, Los Angeles, California

Carroll Meeks, *The Railroad Station*. New Haven: Yale University Press, 1956.

Barbara Flanagan, "Terminal Oasis." *Los Angeles Architect*, February 1980.

Morris Newman, "As the Rest of Downtown Los Angeles Struggles, the Union Station Area Lands Two Big Office Projects." *The New York Times,* August 3, 1994.

Pioneer Courthouse Square, Portland, Oregon

Barbara Walker, *Pioneer Courthouse Square Newsletter,* April 1994.

Randy Gregg, "Pioneer Courthouse Square." *The Oregonian,* April 4, 1994.

Blue Ridge Parkway, Virginia and North Carolina

Harley E. Jolley, *The Blue Ridge Parkway.* Knoxville, Tennessee: The University of Tennessee Press, 1969.

Jim Kerr, "Highway to Heaven." *Sunshine,* August 16, 1992.

Small Towns

Four Towns:

1. Nantucket, Massachusetts

Robert Gambee, *Nantucket Island.* New York: Hastings House Publishers, 1923.

Walter Prichard Eaton, "Nantucket." *The American Mercury,* November 1924.

Edouard A. Stackpole, "Nantucket's 'Summer Place.'" *Cape Cod Compass,* 1969.

Catherine A. Garland, *Nantucket Journeys.* Camden, Maine: Down East Books, 1988.

National Trust for Historic Preservation, "Trust Honors Blair Reeves." *Preservation News,* June 1988.

Howard Mansfield, "New Clout for Historic Districts." *Historic Preservation,* November/December 1988.

2. New Harmony, Indiana

Anne Taylor, *Visions of Harmony.* New York: Oxford University Press, 1987.

Edward K. Spann, *Brotherly Tomorrows.* New York: Columbia University Press, 1989.

Greg Holzhauer, "Best of the Small Towns." *St. Louis Home Magazine,* July 1993.

3. Portsmouth, New Hampshire

Barbara Shea, "Historic Portsmouth Becoming a Popular Spot for Vacationers." *The Times-Union,* June 11, 1995.

Mike McGrail, "A Great Place to Live." *Portsmouth Herald,* August 24, 1995.

4. Greenwich, New York

John Moran, "Greenwich," *Capital,* April 1989.

Greenwich Historical Association and the Washington County Historical Society, *The Historic Walking Tour of Greenwich, New York.* Greenwich, New York, 1992.

Charleston, South Carolina

Pat Conroy, "Shadows of the Old South." *GEO,* Vol. 3, May 1981.

Daniel Cohen, "Charleston's Restoration Challenge." *Historic Preservation,* January/February 1987.

John O'Hagan, "Charleston: A Walk with History." *Southern Living,* March 1988.

Robin Elisabeth Datel, "Southern Regionalism and Historic Preservation in Charleston, South Carolina, 1920-1940." *Journal of Historical Geography,* Vol. 16 No. 2, 1990.

Katherine Ashenburg, "House Proud in Old Charleston." *The New York Times,* March 12, 1995.

Acoma and Taos, New Mexico

Peter Nabokov, *Architecture of the Acoma Pueblo.* Santa Fe: Ancient City Press, 1986.

Vincent Scully, *Pueblo.* Chicago: University of Chicago Press, 1989.

Planned Communities

Yorkship Village, Camden, New Jersey

Richard S. Childs, "The First War Emergency Government Towns for Shipyard Workers." *The Journal of the American Institute of Architects,* May 1918.

Ralph F. Warner, "Yorkship," *The Architectural Review,* June 1918.

"Yorkship Village Auction," *The New York Times,* December 18, 1921.

Edith Elmer Wood, *Recent Trends in American Housing.* New York: The Macmillan Co., 1931.

Mel Scott, *American City Planning Since 1890.* Berkeley: University of California Press, 1969.

Leland Roth, *A Concise History of American Architecture.* New York: Harper and Row, 1979.

Robert Stern, *The Anglo-American Suburb.* New York: St. Martin's Press, 1981.

Patricia Brake et al., *Yorkship Village: Government Subsidized Worker Housing: A University Housing Case Study.* November 21, 1989.

Diggs Town, Norfolk, Virginia

UDA Architects, *The Redesign of Diggs Town.* July 20, 1995.

Seaside, Florida

Phil Patton, "In Seaside, Florida, the Forward Thing is to Look Backward." *Smithsonian Magazine*, Vol. 21, No. 10, January 1991.

Todd W. Bressi, "Planning the American Dream." In: Peter Katz, *The New Urbanism*. New York: McGraw-Hill Inc., 1994.

Endangered and in Transition

Times Square, Manhattan, New York

Ada Louise Huxtable, "Re-inventing Times Square: 1990." In: William R. Taylor, ed., *Inventing Times Square: Commerce and Culture at the Crossroads of the World*. New York: Russell Sage Foundation, 1991.

Gregory F. Gilmartin, *Shaping the City: New York and the Municipal Art Society*. New York: Clarkson Potter, 1995.

Claudia H. Deutsch, "Around Times Square, New Faces at Street Level." *The New York Times*, October 22, 1995.

The French Quarter, New Orleans, Louisiana

Bernard Lemann, *The Vieux Carre—A General Statement*. New Orleans: Tulane University Press, 1966.

Carl Feis, Preface in *Plan and Program for the Preservation of the Vieux Carre*. New Orleans: Vieux Carre Commission, 1968.

The New Orleans Chapter of the American Institute of Architecture, *A Guide to New Orleans Architecture*. New Orleans, Louisiana, 1974.

Coney Island, Brooklyn, New York

John B. Manbeck, *Coney Island Kaleidoscope*. Wilsonville, Oregon: Beautiful America Publishing Company, 1991.

Julie Lasky, "Coney Island, Summer '92." *Print*, Vol. 46, November/December 1992.

Gregory F. Gilmartin, *Shaping the City: New York and the Municipal Art Society*. New York: Clarkson Potter, 1995.

Jacob Riis Park, Queens, New York

Jacob Riis Park Historic District: Historic Structure Report. New York: Gateway, April 1981.

Jacob Riis / Fort Tilden: Development Concept Plan / Environmental Assessment. New York: Gateway, February 1986.

Waterfronts

Oceanfront Walk, Venice, California

Patricia Adler, *A History of the Venice Area*. Los Angeles: L.A. Department of City Planning, 1969.

Horst Schmidt-Brummer, *Venice, California: An Urban Fantasy*. New York: Grossman Publishers, 1973.

Tom Moran, *Fantasy by the Sea*. Culver City, California: Peace Press, Inc., 1980.

John Arthur Maynard, *Venice West*. New Brunswick, New Jersey: Rutgers University Press, 1991.

Ocean Drive, Miami Beach, Florida

Barbara Baer Capitman, *Deco Delights*. New York: E. P. Dutton, 1988.

Beth Dunlop, "Coping with Success." *Historic Preservation*, Vol. 44, No. 4, 1992.

Battery Park City Esplanade, Manhattan, New York

Ken Johnson, "Poetry and Public & Public Service." *Art in America*, Vol. 78, March 1990.

Brendan Gill, "The Sky Line: Battery Park City." *The New Yorker*, August 20, 1990.

Tony Hiss, "At Land's Edge, a Contentment of Light and Shape." *The New York Times*, October 19, 1990.

Paul Goldberger, "Battery Park City's Brave New World." *Architectural Digest*, November 1990.

Susan Tenenbaum, "The Progressive Legacy and the Public Corporation: Enterpreneurship and Public Virtue." *Journal of Policy History*, Vol. 3, No. 3, 1991.

Mac Griswald, "New Urban Parks." *Landscape Architecture*, December 1992.

Abby Bussel, "Simulated City," *P/A*, May 1994.

Main Streets and Places of Commerce

Country Club Plaza, Kansas City, Missouri

Robert Stern, *The Anglo-American Suburb*. New York: St. Martin's Press, 1981.

Richard Longstreth, "J. C. Nichols, the Country Club Plaza, and Notions of Modernity." *Harvard Architectural Review*, Vol. 5, 1986.

Faneuil Hall Marketplace, Boston, Massachusetts

Bernard J. Frieden and Lynne B. Sagalyn, *Downtown, Inc., How America Rebuilds Cities*. Cambridge, Massachusetts: MIT Press, 1989.

Newbury Street, Boston, Massachusetts

Mona Domosh, "Controlling Urban Form: the Development of Boston's Back Bay." *Journal of Historical Geography,* Vol. 18, No. 3, 1992.

Main Street, Madison, Indiana

Robert M. Taylor and John T. Windle, *The Early Architecture of Madison, Indiana.* Indianapolis: Historic Madison, Inc. and Indiana Historical Society, 1986.

Outdoor Living Rooms

Bryant Park, Manhattan, New York

Daniel A. Biederman and Anita R. Nager, "Up From Smoke: A New, Improved Bryant Park?" *New York Affairs,* Vol. 6, No. 4, 1981.

Gregory F. Gilmartin, *Shaping the City: New York and the Municipal Art Society.* New York: Clarkson Potter, 1995.

Mitchell Owens, "Urban Arcadia." *The New York Times Magazine,* October 15, 1995.

Post Office Square, Boston, Massachusetts

Lawrence Bluestone, "A Gift Worthy of Boston." *Boston Business Journal,* May 20, 1991.

Donald Albrecht, "Garden Masquerade." *Architecture,* August 1993.

Urban Land Institute, *Project Reference File,* Vol. 24, No. 3, January-March 1994.

William M. Bulkeley, "Call it Garage Mahal: Lowly Parking Area Becomes Attraction." *The Wall Street Journal,* July 18, 1994.

Washington Square, San Francisco, California

Randolph Delehanty, *San Francisco.* New York: Dial Press, 1988.

Randolph Delehanty, *San Francisco: the Ultimate Guide.* San Francisco: Chronicle Books, 1989.

The Promenade and Plaza, Rockefeller Center, Manhattan, New York

Federal Writers' Project, *New York Panorama.* New York: Random House, 1938.

Carol Herselle Krinsky, *Rockefeller Center.* New York: Oxford University Press, 1970.

Alan Balfour, *Rockefeller Center: Architecture as Theater.* New York: McGraw-Hill, 1978.

William Knowlton Zinsser, *American Places: A Writer's Pilgrimage to 15 of this Country's Most Visited and Cherished Sites.* New York: Harper Collins, 1992.

Low Memorial Library Steps, Columbia University, Manhattan, New York

D. Dean Telfer, "The Evolution of a Modern Campus." *Columbia Today,* Fall 1977.

Paul Venables Turner, *Campus: An American Planning Tradition.* Cambridge, Massachusetts: MIT Press, 1984.

Paul Goldberger, "Cavorting on the Great Urban Staircases." *The New York Times,* August 7, 1987.

Public Squares

The Green, New Haven, Connecticut

Elizabeth Mills Brown, *New Haven: A Guide to Architecture and Urban Design.* New Haven: Yale University Press, 1976.

Rollin Gustav Osterweis, *The New Haven Green and the American Bicentennial.* Hamden, Connecticut: Archon Books, 1976.

Spiro Kostof, *America by Design.* New York: Oxford University Press, 1987.

The Plaza, Santa Fe, New Mexico

Bruce Porter, "Santa Fe." *Connoisseur,* Vol. 218, June 1988.

Vincent Scully, *Pueblo.* Chicago: University of Chicago Press, 1989.

The Historic Santa Fe Foundation, *Old Santa Fe Today.* Albuquerque: University of New Mexico Press, 1991.

El Pueblo de Los Angeles, Los Angeles, California

Antonio Rios-Bustamante, *An Illustrated History of Mexican Los Angeles.* Los Angeles: University of California Press, 1986.

Dolores Hayden, "Placemaking, Preservation and Urban History." *Journal of Architectural Education,* Spring, 1988.

"The Hidden Treasures of El Pueblo de Los Angeles Historic Monument." *Mexican American Sun,* Vol. 44, No. 18, April 30, 1992.

Courthouse Square, Oxford, Mississippi

William Faulkner, *Requiem for a Nun.* New York: Random House, 1975.

Jim Faulkner, *Across the Creek: Faulkner Family Stories.* Jackson, Mississippi: University Press of Mississippi, 1986.

Courthouse Square, Sidney, Ohio

Albert Bush-Brown, *Louis Sullivan.* New York: George Braziller, Inc., 1960.

Dan Becker, *Their Buildings Now.* Sidney, Ohio: Shelby County Chamber of Commerce, 1987.

Lauren S. Weingarden, *Louis H. Sullivan: The Banks.* Cambridge, Massachusetts: The MIT Press, 1987.

Public Buildings

Los Angeles Central Library, Los Angeles, California

Bernadette Dominique Soter, *The Light of Learning: An Illustrated History of the Los Angeles Public Library.* Los Angeles: Library Foundation of Los Angeles, 1993.

John Morris Dixon, "Critique: With All Due Respect." *P/A*, September 1994.

Grand Central Terminal, Manhattan, New York

Gregory F. Gilmartin, *Shaping the City: New York and the Municipal Art Society.* New York: Clarkson Potter, 1995.

South Station, Boston, Massachusetts

Carroll L. V. Meeks, *The Railroad Station.* New Haven, Connecticut: Yale University Press, 1956.

Robert Campbell, "South Station: The Thrill Is Back," *The Boston Globe*, November 21, 1989.

The Atrium, Franklin Institute, Philadelphia, Pennsylvania

Paul Goldberger, "A Born-Again Franklin Institute Banishes Stodginess." *The New York Times*, June 10, 1990.

Margaret Gaskie, "Art for Science." *Architectural Record,* Vol. 179, No. 1, January 1991.

Farmers' Markets

Pike Place Market, Seattle, Washington

John Pastier, "Downtown Seattle Waterfront: Pike Place Market." *Arts + Architecture,* Vol. 4, No. 1, May 1985.

Tim Appelo, "Rescue in Seattle." *Historic Preservation*, Vol. 37, No. 5, October 1985.

Anne Focke, *Sustaining a Vital Downtown Community: A Study of the Market Foundation.* Seattle: The Market Foundation, 1987.

Central Market, Lancaster, Pennsylvania

Stephen Scott, Historical Sketches in Phyllis Pellman Good and Louise Stoltzfus, *The Central Market Cookbook.* Intercourse, Pennsylvania: Good Books, 1989.

Market Square, Roanoke, Virginia

Dave and Louise Hollyer, "Roanoke's City Market." *Virginia,* Vol. 15, No. 2, Fall 1992.

Michael Carlton, "Downtown Roanoke is Really Uptown." *Southern Living,* November 1992.

"There's a Market for the Market." *Roanoke Times & World News*, July 7, 1994.

"Tend to City Market with Care." *Roanoke Times & World News*, July 29, 1994.

Italian Market, Philadelphia, Pennsylvania

Diane Stoneback, "A Taste of Italy." *The Morning Call*, October 9, 1994.

Louise Cianfero Simpson, *History of the Italian Market* (in press).

Turning Points

The Lawn, University of Virginia, Charlottesville, Virginia

Ralph E. Griswold and Frederick Doveton Nichols, *Thomas Jefferson, Landscape Architect.* Charlottesville: University Press of Virginia, 1978.

Lawrence Biemiller, "Planning the College Campus." *The Chronicle of Higher Education,* May 30, 1984.

Richard Guy Wilson, *Thomas Jefferson's Academical Village.* Charlottesville: University Press of Virginia, 1993.

Golden Gate Park, San Francisco, California

Katherine Wilson, *Golden Gate, The Park of a Thousand Vistas.* Caldwell, Idaho: The Caxton Printers, Ltd., 1947.

Federal Writer's Project, *San Francisco.* New York: Hastings House, 1973.

Margot Patterson Doss, *Golden Gate Park at Your Feet.* San Rafael, California: Presidio Press, 1978.

Randolph Delehanty, *San Francisco: the Ultimate Guide.* San Francisco: Chronicle Books, 1989.

Central Park, Manhattan, New York

Walter Karp, "The Central Park." *American Heritage,* Vol. 32, No. 3, 1981.

Elizabeth Blackmar and Roy Rosenzweig, *The Park and the People.* Ithaca: Cornell University Press, 1992.

Joel L. Swerdlow, "Central Park." *National Geographic,* Vol. 183, No. 5, May 1993.

Prospect Park, Brooklyn, New York

William F. Menke and George E. Patton, "Design with Nature and Culture." *Journal of Garden History,* Vol. 2, No. 4, 1982.

Clay Lancaster, *Prospect Park Handbook.* New York: Greensward Foundation, 1988.

Donald E. Simon, "A Plan For All Seasons." *Long Island Historical Journal,* Vol. 3, No. 1, 1990.

Gregory F. Gilmartin, *Shaping the City: New York and the Municipal Art Society.* New York: Clarkson Potter, 1995.

Vietnam Veterans Memorial, Washington, D.C.

Catherine M. Howett, "The Vietnam Veterans Memorial." *Landscape*, Vol. 28, No. 2 , 1985.

John Beardsley, *Earthworks and Beyond: Contemporary Art in the Landscape.* New York: Abbeville Press, 1989.

Oriole Park at Camden Yards, Baltimore, Maryland

"All Aboard the O's Train." *Opening Day: The Newsletter of the Maryland Stadium Authority,* No. 5, March-April 1990, .

"Message from the Executive Director: Why the New Ballpark Makes Dollars and Sense." *Opening Day: The Newsletter of the Maryland Stadium Authority,* No. 11, March-April 1991.

Donald Prowler, "Baltimore Hits Home with New Baseball Park." *PA,* Vol. 73, June 1992.

Tom Ferry, "Classic Ballpark a Hit; A Model for Seattle?" *The Seattle Times,* August 20, 1995.

General Sources and Suggested Readings

Alexander, Christopher, Sara Ishikawa, and Murray Silverstein, *A Pattern Language: Towns, Buildings, Construction.* New York: Oxford University Press, 1977.

Appleyard, Donald, with M. Sue Gerson and Mark Lintell, *Livable Streets.* Berkeley: University of California Press, 1981.

Arendt, Hannah, *The Human Condition.* Chicago: University of Chicago Press, 1989.

Berry, Wendell, *What Are People For?* San Francisco: North Point Press, 1990.

Calthorpe, Peter, Doug Kelbaugh, et al., *The Pedestrian Pocket Book.* Edited by Doug Kelbaugh. New York: Princeton Architectural Press, 1989.

Calthrope, Peter, *The Next American Metropolis: Ecology, Community, and the American Dream.* New York: Princeton Architectural Press, 1993.

Caro, Robert A., *The Power Broker: Robert Moses and the Fall of New York.* New York: Alfred A. Knopf, 1974.

Etzioni, Amitai, *A Responsive Society: Collected Essays on Guiding Deliberate Social Change.* San Francisco: Jossey-Bass Publishers, 1991.

Gilmartin, Gregory F., *Shaping the City: New York and the Municipal Art Society.* New York: Clarkson Potter/Publishers, 1995.

Gratz, Roberta Brandes, *The Living City.* New York: Simon & Schuster, 1989.

Hall, Peter, *Cities of Tomorrow: An Intellectual History of Urban Planning and Design in the Twentieth Century.* Cambridge: Basil Blackwell, 1990.

Hegemann, Werner, and Elbert Peets, *The American Vitruvius.* Edited by Alan J. Plattus. Reprint. New York: Princeton Architectural Press, 1988.

Hiss, Tony, *The Experience of Place.* New York: Alfred A. Knopf, 1990.

Jacobs, Jane, *The Death and Life of Great American Cities.* New York: Random House, 1993.

Kalfus, Melvin, *Frederick Law Olmsted: The Passion of a Public Artist.* New York: New York University Press, 1990.

Katz, Peter, *The New Urbanism: Toward an Architecture of Community.* New York: McGraw-Hill, Inc., 1994.

Kemmis, Daniel, *Community and the Politics of Place.* Oklahoma: University of Oklahoma, 1990.

Kostof, Spiro, *America by Design.* New York: Oxford University Press, 1987.

Kunstler, James Howard, *The Geography of Nowhere: The Rise and Decline of America's Man-made Landscape.* New York: Simon & Schuster, 1993.

Langdon, Philip, with Robert Shibley and Polly Welch, *Urban Excellence.* New York: Bruner Foundation, 1990.

Langdon, Philip, *A Better Place to Live: Reshaping the American Suburb.* Amherst, Massachusetts: University of Massachusetts, 1994.

Lennard, Suzanne H. Crowhurst, and Henry L. Lennard, *Public Life in Urban Places.* New York: Gondolier Press, 1984.

Lennard, Suzanne H. Crowhurst, and Henry L. Lennard, *Livable Cities Observed.* New York: Gondolier Press, 1984.

Mumford, Lewis, *The City in History.* New York: Harcourt, Brace & World, 1961.

Newman, Oscar, *Defensible Space: Crime Prevention Through Urban Design.* New York: Macmillan Publishing Co., 1973.

Oldenburg, Ray, *The Great Good Place: Cafes, Coffee Shops, Community Centers. Beauty Parlors, General Stores, Bars, Hangouts and How They Get You Through the Day.* New York: Paragon House, 1991.

Rudofsky, Bernard, *Streets for People: A Primer for Americans*. Garden City, New York: Doubleday, 1969.

Scully, Vincent, *Pueblo: Mountain, Village, Dance*. 2nd ed., Chicago: University of Chicago Press, 1989.

Shaffer, Carolyn R., and Kristin Anundsen, *Creating Community Anywhere: Finding Support and Connection in a Fragmented World*. New York: Putnam, 1993.

Stein, Clarence S., *Toward New Towns for America*. 3d ed. Cambridge: MIT Press, 1966.

Stern, Robert A. M., and John Montague Massengale, guest eds., *Architectural Design Profile. The Anglo-American Suburb*. London: Architectural Design, 1981.

Stern, Robert A. M., Gregory Gilmartin, and John Massengale, *New York 1900: Metropolitan Architecture and Urbanism 1890-1915*. New York: Rizzoli, 1983.

Stern, Robert A. M., Gregory Gilmartin, and Thomas Mellins, *New York 1930: Architecture and Urbanism between the Two World Wars*. New York: Rizzoli, 1987.

Sucher, David, *City Comforts: How to Build an Urban Village*. Seattle: City Comforts Press, 1995.

Whyte, William H., *City: Rediscovering the Center*. Garden City, New York: Doubleday, 1988.

About the Author

Gianni Longo is an architect and urban-planning consultant based in New York. Born in Italy, he studied and lived in Venice and Rome before moving to the United States, in 1971. This book is the result of his many years of work with major American cities, particularly Chattanooga, Tennessee, where, in 1984, he designed and implemented Vision 2000, a citizens involvement program largely credited for that city's renaissance. Longo lectures extensively on the public places and public life of cities.